PANGOLINS

in my life

Book Design – Jessica Willemse
Publishing Coordinator – Sharon Kizziah-Holmes

Paperback-Press
an imprint of Paperback Press, LLC
Springfield, Missouri, USA

ISBN -13:978-1-956806-97-7

PANGOLINS

in my life

by Maria Diekmann

"

Note from the author

by Maria Diekmann

I hope that, through this book, I can in some way help you to learn more about one of the most ancient, fascinating, and little-known creatures alive today. What you will read is my story with pangolins.

2

I do not profess to be an expert on all eight species, nor can I honestly say that I know everything there is to know about my specialty—the Temminck's ground pangolin, *Smutsia temminckii*. I am sure the time will come when we know more facts and figures, but for now much of what I share is a combination of years of observation, data collected from our team, and some guessing.

I could have waited another decade to share this story and had more scientific backing, but by then pangolins could be extinct. And many more books would have been published with incorrect information. It is a disturbing phenomenon to me that so many books have published "facts" that are nothing of the sort. So little is truly known about these shy, elusive creatures that once an assumption is printed, it is considered a reliable truth when often it is not. Confusion is added when researchers from different habitats report their observations because, at least within Namibian borders, there may be unique behaviours and biological differences due to the extreme aridness of the environment.

I am going to focus this book on Temminck's pangolins or ground pangolins as this is the species I have worked with the most and the only one found in Namibia, Africa, where I lived. Any reference in my information to "pangolin," unless otherwise named, is referring to them. Unless I specifically refer to another country, I am basing all my information on those found in Namibia.

I am confident that not everyone in the world will agree with my theories, approach to conservation nor methods, but that has never been my goal. My overriding concern is the conservation of pangolins, and I know in my heart that any mistakes I made were done unintentionally and with the best knowledge available at the time. That is enough for me to look in the mirror and live with myself. Experience has shown me that strong women are often either loved or hated. I am neither a saint nor a demon, just a normal person doing the work I love with determination, dedication, and passion. If the thoughts in this book cause you concern, then my best suggestion is not to read it.

For those who do enjoy this book, I hope it adds insight into the little knowledge we do have and shares information in a casual, fun, and educational way—half storytelling and half "My Observations." In the future, my theories may be proven correct or not, but I hope that sharing them at least ignites a journey toward awareness. If you enjoy the following pages, I will consider my aims a success.

- Love, Maria

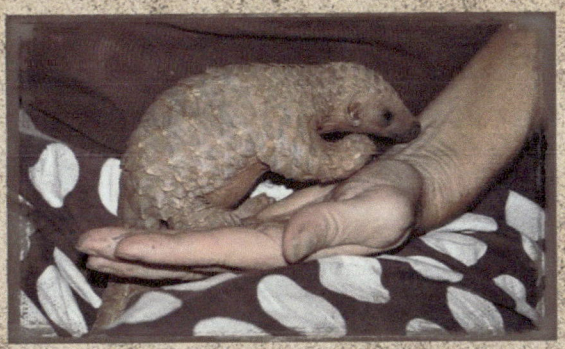

"

How the world learned about pangolins

When I started working with pangolins, very few people knew what one was. Even my conservation colleagues often asked me why I was working with "penguins" in the bush. Since those early days, pangolins have reached the world's attention. I attribute this to six main events.

1. Several first world countries decided to provide funding to stop the illegal trade in rhino and elephant, and once cargo ships were inspected, thousands of tons of pangolin scales were discovered. These seizures allowed researchers to prove that the sheer numbers confiscated meant our wild populations were on the brink of extinction.

2. In 2012, Sir David Attenborough listed the pangolin in the top ten species he hoped would be saved from extinction.

3. His Royal Highness William Prince of Wales gave an impassioned speech in 2016 mentioning the illegal trafficking of rhino, elephant, lion, and pangolin, and the world said, "Rhino, elephant, lion, and what?"

4. Leading conservation bodies recognized the problem and reacted by publicly declaring the pangolin the MOST ILLEGALLY TRAFFICKED ANIMAL IN THE WORLD, and in 2016 history was made when all eight pangolin species were moved from CITES Appendix II to Appendix I, disallowing any trade without a permit for research or legal purposes. This is not usually the headline wanted for an animal you are trying to protect, but in this case, it brought immediate attention to a creature in dire need of publicity. The media took note and headlined stories describing the most illegally trafficked animal in the world that could go extinct before we even know much about it. Soon the mass public was curious.

5. In 2018, BBC aired the first full-length pangolin nature documentary called "Pangolins: The World's Most Wanted Animal" and brought their plight to the attention of millions. The iconic Sir David Attenborough narrated the UK version, and people were spellbound by the story of our own Honey Bun and how she brought to life the character of these shy, sweet creatures. The film won recognition, awards, and was hailed as a huge boost to pangolin conservation.

6. In 2020, the coronavirus COVID-19 hit the world, and the first reports linked pangolins as the possible transmitters of the virus from bats to humans. Since then, these initial reports have come under severe scrutiny, and the data no longer strongly supports the link. I have heard reports that, in fact, no pangolins were found at the Wuhan wet market where the outbreak may have begun, but as they say, "no publicity is bad publicity," and the word pangolin reached the world once again.

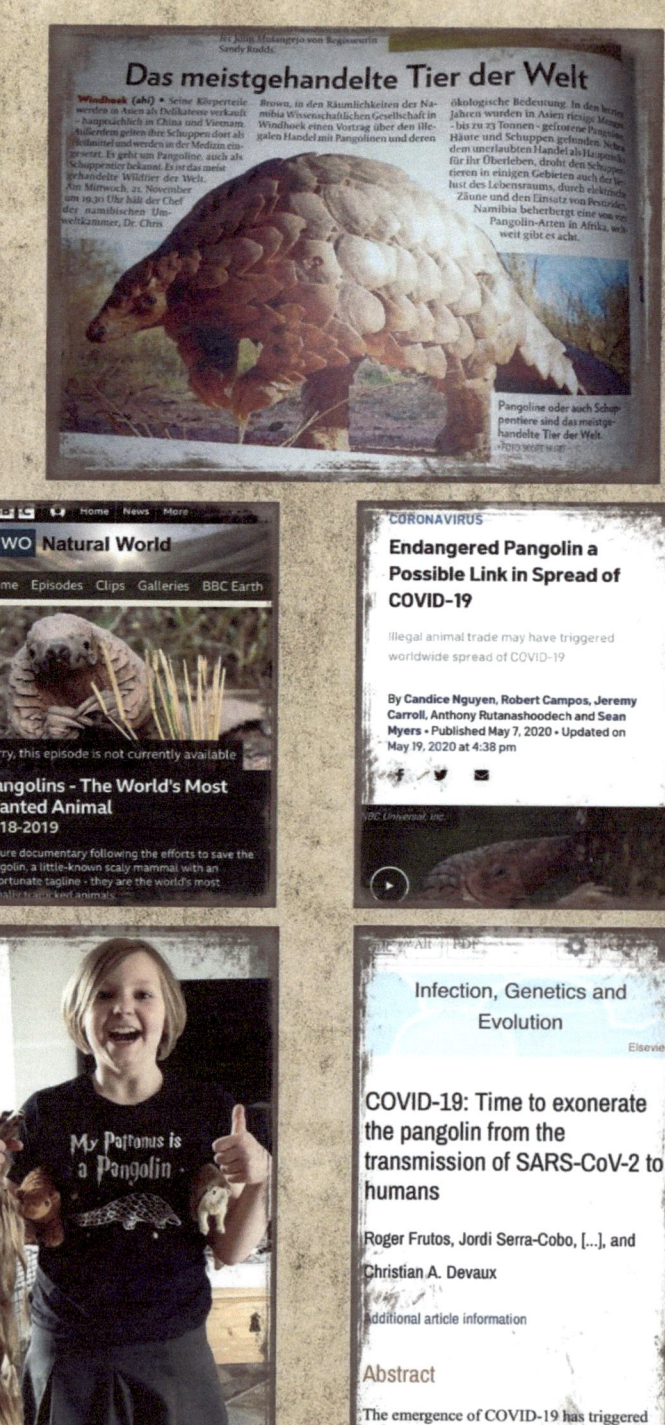

In the past few years, pangolin awareness has grown. Artwork appeared on buildings, canvases, and magazines; books for all ages were published; poets became prophetic; and young people fundraised through bake sales, dressed up like pangolins for Halloween, and began educating their neighbours and friends. Leading movie stars like Jackie Chan and Angelababy joined organizations like WildAid to champion campaigns in Asia, and legislators and law enforcement agencies began developing and delivering harsher penalties for illegal trade. Even Disney films finally gave the pangolin its first speaking role in a major studio film with the adaptation of *The Jungle Book*. All this attention also attracted a new wave of young scientists and conservationists.

"

The eight pangolin species

There are eight species of pangolins, and all of them are mammals, which makes them the only truly scaly mammal in the world; four are found in Asia and the remaining in Africa.

Asia

Species: **Chinese Formosan pangolin**
Latin name: *Manis pentadactyla*
IUCN listing: **Critically endangered**

Species: **Sunda or Malayan pangolin**
Latin name: *Manis javanica*
IUCN listing: **Critically endangered**

Species: **Indian or thick-tailed pangolin**
Latin name: *Manis crassicaudata*
IUCN listing: **Endangered**

Species: **Philippine or Palawan pangolin**
Latin name: *Manis culionensis*
IUCN listing: **Critically endangered**

Africa

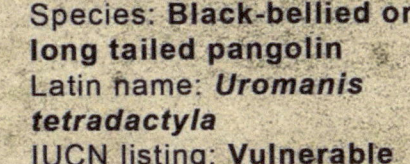

Species: **White-bellied or tree pangolin**
Latin name: *Phataginus tricuspis*
IUCN listing: **Endangered**

Species: **Black-bellied or long tailed pangolin**
Latin name: *Uromanis tetradactyla*
IUCN listing: **Vulnerable**

Species: **Giant or giant ground pangolin**
Latin name: *Smutsia giganea*
IUCN listing: **Endangered**

Species: **Ground, Cape, or Temminick's pangolin**
Latin name: *Smutsia temminckii*
IUCN listing: **Vulnerable**

All Asian species and two found in Africa are tree pangolins. They tend to be smaller, thinner, have longer tails, back foot claws, and longer front foot claws to help them grasp branches and climb trees, and some have long hairs growing between their scales. My experience in Asia was a brief visit to Save Vietnam's Wildlife, but there are several other organizations that have done ground-breaking conservation work.

Firsthand observations and consultations have led me to conclude that, for a variety of reasons, the care and rehabilitation of tree pangolins is easier than that of ground pangolins and probably the giant pangolin. Although still incredibly fragile, they appear to be more adaptable to food sources-stronger and less stressed when captured or injured.

The two species that live mainly on the ground are only found in Africa. The seldom seen giant pangolin is believed to live in remote areas of central Africa, and the ground pangolin is found in southern, central, and eastern Africa. Ground pangolins are considered by many to be one of the most difficult animals in the world to raise and care for in captivity. It is the only one of the eight species that can survive in an arid environment, and animals that have this adaptation tend to be more difficult to care for in a captive situation. The previous list names all species, with the smallest black-bellied pangolin at about 80 cm long (31.5 inches) and the giant pangolin recorded to reach up to 1.8 metres (5.9 feet). As you can see, not one has managed to retain only one common name. I have no idea why, but after consulting with various colleagues, I have recorded what I believe are the preferred common names first. This leaves me in a bit of a dilemma with the very species I focus on in Namibia, as I have always preferred referring to it as the easily pronounced and remembered Cape pangolin.

However, in 2019, the IUCN (International Union for Conservation of Nature) pangolin group, with leadership from South African conservationists, made a decision to officially change the Cape pangolin name to Temminck's ground pangolin. As they say, a name is just a name, so in my duty to a respectful scientific approach, I am obliged to refer to my Cape pangolin as a Temminck's ground pangolin from a science perspective, but for ease in this book, I will simply refer to them as ground pangolins in the following chapters. As far as I could determine, their Latin name was also changed in 2009 from Manis temminckii to Smutsia temminckii, retaining the last name of Dutch zoologist Coenraad Jacob Temminck.

Temminck was born in 1778 and ran the National Natural History Museum at Leiden. He has several species—including sharks, fish, reptiles, birds, and mammals—named after him, and it appears these honors came more from his financial and institutional history than any hands-on work with most of them.

IUCN listings are the official determination on the status of how many pangolins are left in the world, and each species is classified as either least concern, near threatened, vulnerable, endangered, or critically endangered. Up until 2013, the Temminck's pangolin was listed as "least concern" due to lack of data proving otherwise. This status made it difficult to apply for critical funding, but fortunately the classification was quickly upgraded to "vulnerable" once their plight gained attention. Many argue they should follow in the steps of their Asian counterparts and be upgraded to "endangered" or "critically endangered" due to the speed and extent of increased illegal trafficking. Field data is not extensive enough to prove the massive declines, but I would argue that the continued confiscation of thousands of tons of illegally trafficked African pangolin scales does and therefore warrants an immediate upgrade.

"

The history of REST

In the year 2000, I started an organization called the Rare & Endangered Species Trust (REST) and focused on the Forgotten Five.

The Forgotten Five

Cape vulture
Gyps coprotheres

Spotted rubber frog
Phrynomantis affinis

Dwarf python
Python anchietae

Damara dik-dik
Madoqua kirkii

Temminck's ground pangolin
Smutsia temminckii

What most do not know is that I almost called it NEST—Namibian Endangered Species Trust. Our flagship species from the start was the Cape griffon or Cape vulture—*Gyps coprotheres* (yet another animal with two common names). It is the most endangered species in Namibia, and I argue that vultures are the most important animals in Africa due to their ability to consume and thus dispose of diseased dead animals (but that is another book). I knew from the start I wanted to protect biodiversity and not just focus on one animal, and NEST made most people think only of birds. So I decided on REST.

At the time, I was a farm wife raising two children. I was born and educated in the United States, and one side of my family was very involved in law and politics, particularly in defeating the American racial laws of the 1950s. I envisioned my life would follow my family's lead, and I had come to southern Africa in 1989 to look at the political situation firsthand. Mr. Nelson Mandela was still in prison, and apartheid was just crumbling. However, I met the man of my dreams within hours of landing, accepted work at a local law firm, married three years later, and began a family. Everything that happened after, both wonderful and tragic, led me to where I am today, and for that I will always be grateful.

REST soon became a world leader in vulture conservation and was the first to put satellite trackers on vultures in Africa. Based on our interest in biodiversity, we chose five flagship species, with one eventually being changed from the African wild dog, *Lycaon pictus*, to Damara dik-dik, *Madoqua kirkii*, for various reasons. Twenty-three years later, I have watched as these species I called the "Forgotten Five" went from seldom noticed to a state where three of the five are now gaining world attention for all the wrong reasons.

The Cape griffon, Temminck's pangolin, and spotted rubber frog, *Phrynomantis affinis*, are all believed to be highly endangered. We still know very little about the Damara dik-dik and dwarf python, *Python anchietae*, but it can be reasonably assumed that populations are declining due to unethical hunting and illegal trade. With that brief history, we arrive at the beginning of my love affair with pangolins.

15

16

"

My first pangolins

From 2000-2010, three pangolins passed through the REST center, and I remember each one in detail. The first was found on a public road near a community that would have killed it for meat or money.

Two decades after the fact, I admit I made some major handling mistakes, but thank goodness, nothing critical. It dug a burrow in the vulture aviary and remained rolled in a ball for most of the two days it stayed with us. What I did not know at the time was that, had the pangolin been more inquisitive, it could have climbed the link fencing, likely fallen, and caused itself serious injury. Pangolins are expert climbers when in danger, and I give them all the middle name Houdini for their ability to escape from the most unlikely places. At the time, I contacted the only researcher I could find and was informed that, contrary to popular belief, they did not hibernate in winter and I should let him go in a remote area of our farm, which we did immediately.

The second pangolin came in years later from the police. By the time I arrived at the station late one night, much of the night shift was sitting on top of their desks with a wild pangolin roaming freely around the station. It was not a question of bravery, but the officers had no idea how to respond as nothing had prepared them for this strange creature that had shredded the cardboard box he was held in. I scooped the pangolin up, kept him overnight in an animal room, and released him in a secure area of a new farm where I was living, having just gone through a divorce.

My third release was caught by a well-meaning neighbor. He knew I talked about pangolins to school groups and farmers, found one while traveling through a riverbed, and brought me a "gift." I felt horrible, kindly convinced the farmer to give me the exact location, and released it back in its territory within hours. Due to lack of better knowledge, if a pangolin was found, the protocol that most conservationists used at the time was:

• Weigh it.
• Use a straight ruler moved around the outside edge of the body to try to measure length (a useless scientific method).
• Put a bowl of water in front of it while organizing transport.
• No talking.
• No touching.
• Put it in a clean animal box for transport.
• Take it to the most remote area you know and release it.

These actions were all well-meant and believed to be in the best interest of the animal. Since then, we have learned so much more about the care of this sensitive creature, and it is frustrating that many who work with pangolins still follow these ancient protocols, even though improved methods should now be the norm. We still do not have all the answers, but there is definite progress.

19

"

Roxy - The pangolin that changed my life

The year was 2012, and the time was midafternoon. I received a call from a friend and businessman in a local town. There was a gentleman at his work asking for help to save a pangolin.

He was a Chinese national living in Namibia, and Namibians had come into his shop selling the pangolin for N$400.00 (about $26.00 USD). He bought it out of pity for the animal and was offering it free to anyone who could help secure its safety. At the time, I had a small house in town, so I took the pangolin there in case we needed to be close to veterinary care as the sellers had told the buyer that they had carried her around for a week trying to sell her. I will never forget my absolute awe as she climbed out of the box, calmly walked to the water, started drinking, and when finished proceeded to walk straight toward me and sniff around my legs. No pangolin I had ever heard of or seen had been so calm after such trauma. I knew immediately this pangolin was special, and within hours we were trying to get a tracker so we could monitor her after release into the wild. As a close friend searched the internet for a tracker we could courier, she also discovered posts from a woman in Zimbabwe who had cared for two ground pangolins for several years. I immediately called, and thus began a close friendship with a woman I have still never met in person.

Roxy Dankwerts of Wild Is Life sanctuary in Zimbabwe became my lifeline then and months later. She shared private "tricks" she felt calmed pangolins and gave me the moral support needed to feel I could manage. It seemed only fitting I name the new pangolin Roxy. Roxy pangolin and I formed an immediate bond. We moved to the farm, she began to forage on walks in the bush, and I gave myself six days in total to secure a tracker or release her without one.

Day 4 began like each day before. The previous night I had taken Roxy pang to the neighbor's land as they had some cleared areas for their wildlife, and it was easier to follow her while she foraged. We were all amazed at how bonded to me the pangolin seemed to be, and no one noticed anything physically out of the ordinary. Late the next morning, I entered the vulture hide where I had chosen to let her stay as it had a dirt floor, little internal light, and was very quiet. Some visitors had joined on the condition that no one would speak a word or take a picture, and I assured them they would just see a ball in the corner. But it was a very special ball and momentous opportunity. Little did I know how momentous!

My volunteer at the time and I entered first, and I immediately realized something was wrong. Roxy shuffled out to me, and as I sat, she curled right up in my lap. Looking closely, terror suddenly ran through my veins as I saw what appeared to be a snake curled up inside her belly area. My immediate thought was, "Well, Maria, she has been bitten, and you are going to receive your first snake bite." It all happened so quickly that it took me a few more seconds to realize the truth. I handed my phone to the volunteer and asked her to start filming as we realized Roxy pang had just given birth. Immediately, everyone was asked to leave. I shifted Roxy and baby, still attached by the umbilical cord, into the dirt hollow she had been sleeping in and was amazed as she allowed me to film the after birth of her baby for a few minutes before leaving them. Later, we named the little boy Katiti, meaning "small one" in the local Herero language. It was a day I will never forget.

"

Mating

As far as I know, no one has properly documented how pangolins mate. I have read many humorous accounts in various books, but for the life of me I cannot figure out how the authors believe it is possible in the ways they describe.

26

Some describe the male mounting the female from behind, as if the observer did not notice there are several hard scales preventing such a position. I have seen mating twice in the bush and numerous times in a unique captive situation. In the wild, based on two similar events, the male was drawn toward the female from hundreds of meters away, probably through scent. He approached her from behind, and they began the courtship. She was not particularly interested and tried to run away. He followed and kept putting his front foot out, trying to trip up her back legs. Eventually, she stopped, and he climbed over her back from the side, quickly got underneath, and copulated from below. He was then upside down underneath her in the position of a cross, with their stomachs touching. This took only seconds, and then she left.

In captivity, breeding took much longer and went on for an hour or two almost daily for just over a month. During my observations, copulation occurred every evening after the pangolins had eaten, drunk water, and would normally have settled for the night. His penis was erect, but I never tried to get close enough to see copulation as I did not want to disturb them. I have only observed this captive mating in a male and female that already had an existing strong bond, and both felt at home with their captivity. Their continuous rolling together could have been perceived as aggression by a casual observer, and I do believe dominance and aggressive behavior is similar. However, in these instances the intertwined rolling only happened during this short period of time, and the intention was obvious to anyone who knows pangolin behavior. I personally believe that mating in captivity is incredibly rare. The circumstances, relationships, and environment must be ideal, and for this reason, captive breeding of this species for research, conservation, or trade is virtually impossible.

Observations as I know them

• Males and females have definitive genitalia, and although the testes of a male are not as noticeable as in most mammals, it becomes more obvious with experience.
• The male's penis will always become erect when the animal is under sedation, at least with isoflurane.
• Males and females may sleep together during the breeding season.
• Strong bonds can be formed between male and female pairs.
• I believe they are exclusive to their partners from year to year simply because he holds a territory near her, and in exceptional cases, if they form a strong bond, they may mate repeatedly over the years.
• I believe she will change partners if another male takes over the territory or is passing through undetected by the dominant male and happens upon the female in heat.
• I believe that females may be physically mature enough at two years of age to breed, but they only become young adults at the age of three and thus do not normally give birth until almost four years of age. Males probably are fully mature by five but can start breeding at three years old.

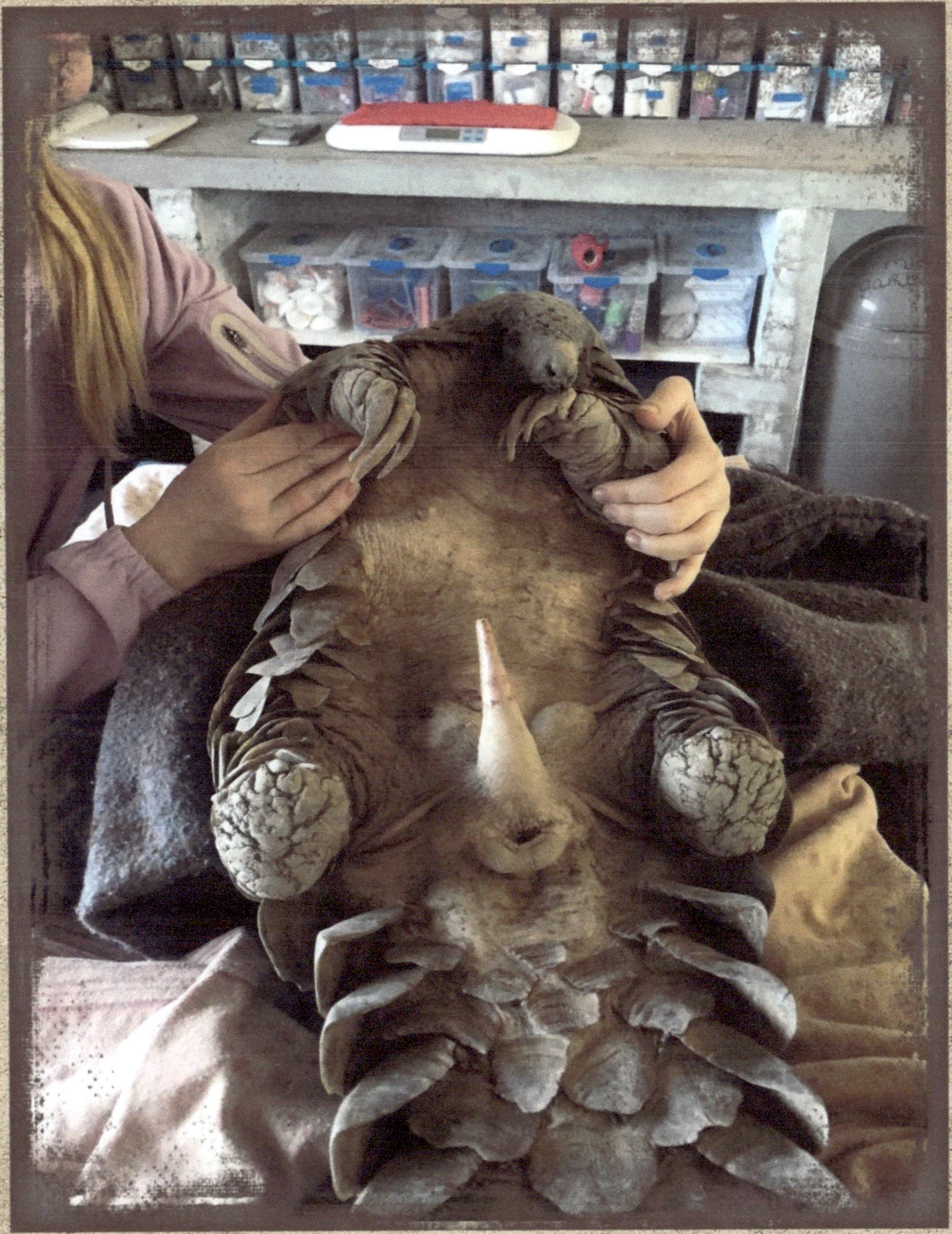

Male

Female

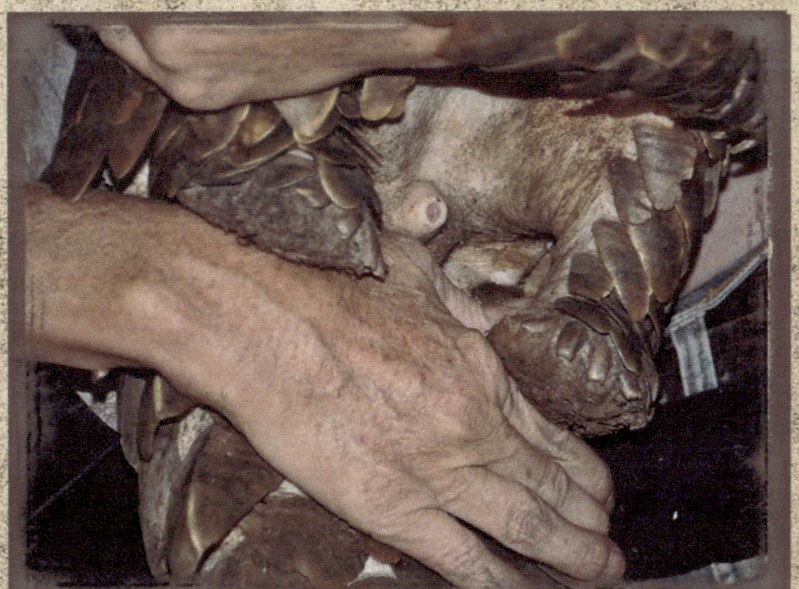

Male

28

" Pregnancy and birth

What happened after Roxy gave birth was one of the biggest adventures of my life. Now unable to release a new mother into an unknown territory, we decided it was best to provide her and her pup with a home until releasable.

By this time, Roxy pang and I were very close, and I moved a mattress into her hide and started recording every moment. I lived what I called vampire hours and felt like the mother of a newborn, napping whenever I got a chance. As a conservationist, I relished the insights I was getting into pangolin life, and as a scientist, I was meticulous in recording the time and duration of every activity.

As you can imagine, this did not allow for much nighttime sleep. Because we could find no one who had ever experienced such a unique situation, I worried that if Roxy did not go out in the bush to feed on demand, she would lose her milk. Usually between ten pm and two am she would go to the hide door, and within moments one could find me with a headlamp facing forward for light—and one facing back for security—stumbling through the thorn bush, trying desperately to keep up with my much smaller and mobile friend. Anyone who has ever visited Namibia knows the bush in the central region is very thick thorn bush of various species and almost impossible to get through during the day, let alone at night. However, I was determined to make this a success. I can now admit I simply do not know how I managed, and I am not sure I could do it again.

Up until he was two and a half months old, Roxy would usually curl around Katiti when sleeping, and you could hear him suckling milk. As he got bigger, he started sleeping rolled up next to her, but continued to drink. Occasionally, she would bring him and both would sleep curled up next to me. Pangolins have two mammary glands, like elephants and humans, but we still do not know for how long they continue suckling in nature because Katiti was still suckling when Roxy left at eleven weeks and four days. I suspect about three and a half to four months, and they may occasionally drink for another month or two in the evenings.

Roxy, Katiti, and I continued this way of life from October 24th until January 12th, and a number of times she took Katiti on her feeding expeditions, although he never ate. She would carry him for a while, and when he fell off under a branch or over a rock, she would often turn and wait for him to climb up on her back. However, sometimes she continued walking, as if she expected I would fetch him and bring him along. Whether I disturbed her natural instincts or whether she just trusted me to carry him home out of convenience, I can never be sure.

In an effort to help others around the world understand pangolin pups better, I was asked by a leading world animal organization to share photos of Roxy and Katiti, since I was sharing the first public photos of a mother and pup. As an example of how little was known at the time, I had sent a series of pictures of Katiti climbing onto her back. Only one was used publicly, and it soon caused major misinformation. The photo used showed Katiti just as he was crawling up mama's tail, and soon books were publishing the "fact" that grounds' pups rode on their mothers' tails like their Asian counterparts. But of course this is not true as the ground pangolins walk mainly on their hinds legs so would be off balance with such a weight on their tails. It does not seem possible that we knew so little only ten years ago and that misinformation could spread so rapidly and easily.

Then, one day, the unexpected happened. It had been raining for days, and Roxy had not been able to forage as much as usual. My volunteer and I brought her back after sunset but knew she was still hungry. Roxy learned early on that if she wanted anything, she would come up to my legs, stand on her hind legs, put her two front feet near my knees, and look me straight in the eye. I would rub her tummy, pick her up to go home, or just hold her in my arms. Instinctively, I always knew what she wanted, and she responded with gratitude and trust.

That evening is one burned in my memory. We came in, and I sat on the cement bench I used as a bed. She approached me, did her begging, and I remember turning to the volunteer and saying she wanted to go out again because she was still hungry. There had been three evenings during those early months in which I had lost her in the night, and she had always returned by morning to care for Katiti. We still had not been able to find a tracker for her, but everyone who met her believed she was so bonded with both me and Katiti that she would never leave willingly.

Based on these assumptions, I made the decision to let her go out on her own, sure that I would see her in a few hours. I took her to a nearby tree, watched her start up the hill, and to my deepest regret, I never saw her again. Days of searching and calling followed because I now had a healthy 1.786 pup to care for who had only drunk his mother's milk up until then.

Again, I frantically called Roxy in Zimbabwe as Katiti lost weight and condition. A volunteer eventually got him to dig for some ants, but it was never enough to sustain him. I began to neglect my personal care and was losing weight along with Katiti. One day while holding him in my arms, I grabbed a packet of crackers and sour cream and ate just to sustain myself. The next thing I knew, Katiti was licking sour cream from the bowl. A quick call to Roxy to find out what she thought, and I will never forget her words. "If he's eating anything . . . just let him. It can't be worse than nothing."

And so it began that Katiti stabilized, got strong enough to start feeding himself in the wild, had a tracking device fitted, and became a success story. Eventually, Katiti foraged 100% for his own food, but until the day he went wild at just over three years old, if I wanted to give him a treat a few times a year, it would be a spoonful of sour cream. Funny enough, no pangolin since then has ever liked it.

To this day, no one has been able to prove the length of pregnancy in a ground pangolin. It drives me crazy that one book will assure you it is three months while others will state that gestation is four, five, or six months. I have no idea who provides these "facts," but they seem to appear out of nowhere. My guess is six to nine months, leaning toward nine.

Roxy Dankwerts assures me she has cared for two adult females, who had no contact with males at her center, and both gave birth at around eight months, which would prove those females came in pregnant and gestation can be much longer than most believe.

34

Roxy pang left Katiti at approximately three months. In the week before she left, I recorded a lot of behavior that, looking back, resembles scent marking in the grass. Could she have been in heat and looking for a mate? Is that why she left her baby that night, or did she have an untimely accident? We will probably never know, but my gut says she came into heat and probably would have taken her baby in normal circumstances. Unfortunately, at the time most researchers believed that a pup stayed with its mom for up to a year, so we thought there was plenty of time before any separation would naturally occur. If so, she could have returned for him, but she never did.

I would have done some things differently if I had known then what I know now, but unfortunately, at that time there was no precedence since we were the first to publicly witness a birth, record an amazing mother's care, and then have a sudden unexpected departure. Many believe that must be one of the most exciting opportunities for a researcher, but honestly, I consider myself a conservationist first and a researcher second. I will admit it was just plain terrifying, and I longed for advice.

Within Roxy's first minutes of delivery, we were already defying the first "fact" found in most books. Infant ground pangolins are not normally born with soft, pink scales that harden in the first few days. It is hard to say who first came up with that observation, but I believe once it was printed others just reprinted it. Full-term baby ground pangolins are born with hard grey or brownish scales. Based on a documented number of full-term and premature births, I believe the theory of soft, pink scales came from observations of premature births that often occurred in captivity due to the mother's stress. She may even abort early if she feels she and her pup are under severe threat or by mothers with less birthing experience that find themselves suddenly surrounded by humans.

Pangolins do not generally like people and seldom get accustomed to captivity. Often, they prefer to roll up in a ball and starve themselves rather than eat a captive diet, even under good care conditions. As a result, no zoo in the world has managed to keep a ground pangolin in captivity long-term.

In my experience, most pangolin mothers are very protective of their young. I believe they only have one pup either yearly or every two years. Of the six pup births or infants I have witnessed, all the mothers except two were instantly bonded with their pups. In the first of the nonbonding mamas, it was obvious there were contributing factors.

The story started with a brave woman named Yvonne, living on the Namibian side of the border with Angola. She was approached by a local to buy a pangolin, contacted the authorities, and in a successful police operation, the pangolin was rescued on August 21, 2013. Unknown to the conservation officer who took her home for the night, the pangolin was highly pregnant, and the intense stress forced her to go into labor prematurely. When he approached her the following morning, she had already delivered a pup. I received an urgent call to come as fast as I could and took my assistant so she could help me care for the animals on the long drive back.

Imagine our surprise upon arrival to learn that a decision had been made by conservation authorities to release the mother and pup back into the wild the following day, regardless of their obvious need for immediate veterinary care. To this day I believe those initial decisions were made based on lack of proper information, but I couldn't believe my ears. We spent the entire night contacting anyone we could think of, trying to change the decision while still finding time to bottle feed the pup and allowing the mama to relax.

Upon careful inspection that evening, I realized the mother's front foot was badly bruised and probably broken, and she was still bleeding from her uterus. There was no chance either would survive if released. Because we had been allowed to care for the pangolins overnight, we were able to establish that legal possession was ours.

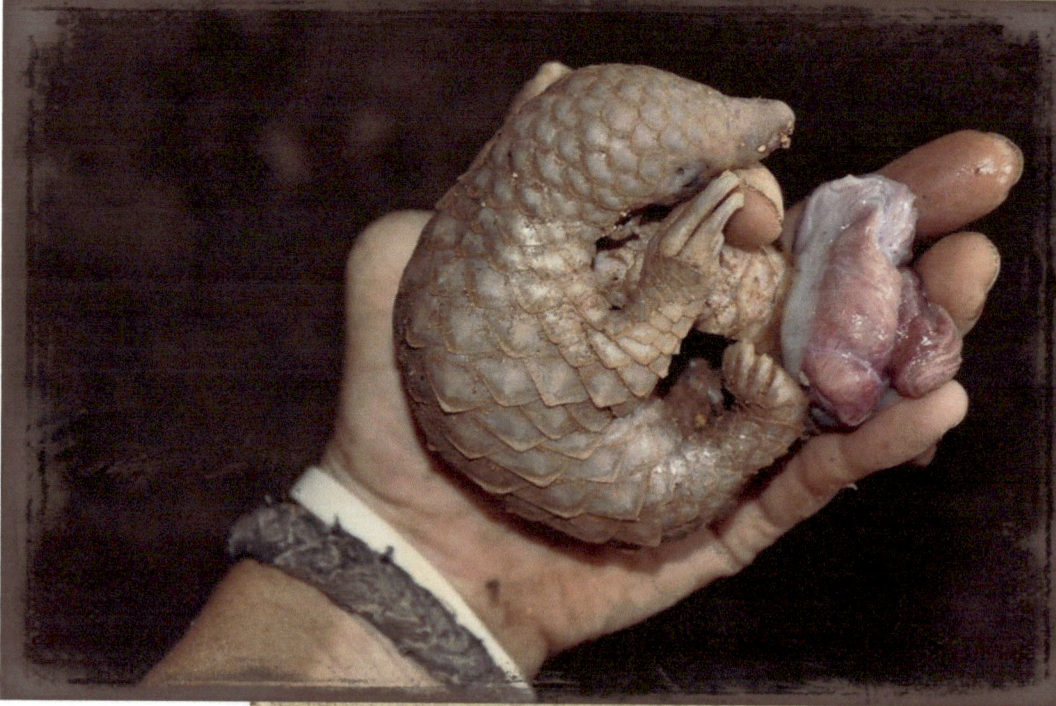

37

When I rushed to an attorney for legal advice, he reiterated that the Namibian constitution not only allowed but required me to provide veterinary care for any animal needing it that was in my care, if I could provide such care. What ensued over the next six hours was a battle over their fate that entailed one official physically threatening my young assistant, me racing around in a vehicle with a bleeding pangolin, trying to avoid detection, and thankfully, eventually someone with higher authority allowing me to take authorized possession and rush my two new charges to the vet.

Sadly, soon afterward both died one day after another. The little boy was the first infant pangolin that I held dead in the palm of my hand, but regrettably, he would not be the last. Colleagues worried that I had unnecessarily "burnt bridges" with local authorities for two pangolins I knew had little hope of survival, but my heart and soul could not have allowed anything different. To this day I am content with my actions in this case.

Abandonment was tragically what happened with the second unsuccessful birth. This "bad" mother we named Talia was younger and most likely a first-time mama. She had absolutely no interest in the baby, and I believe she didn't know what to do and had been through so much trauma that she panicked. This case was interesting because the mama pangolin was kept at REST for a month before giving birth. With only two previous births as an example, I already had a gut feeling there was a birthing season and it had precedence and made sense that food supply and rains would determine the best survival rate of a baby. Katiti had been born on October 20, 2012, and the second pup prematurely on August 21, 2013, so that began to define the birthing season.

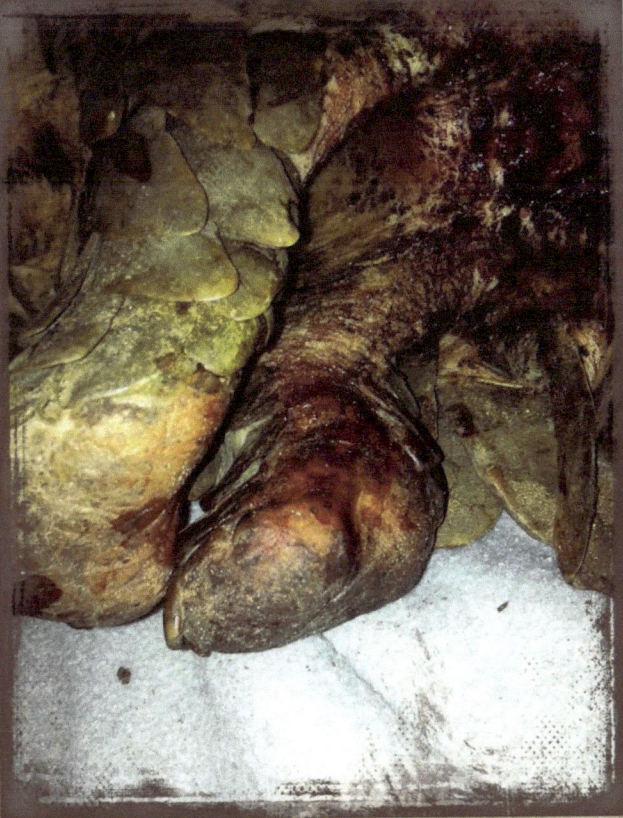
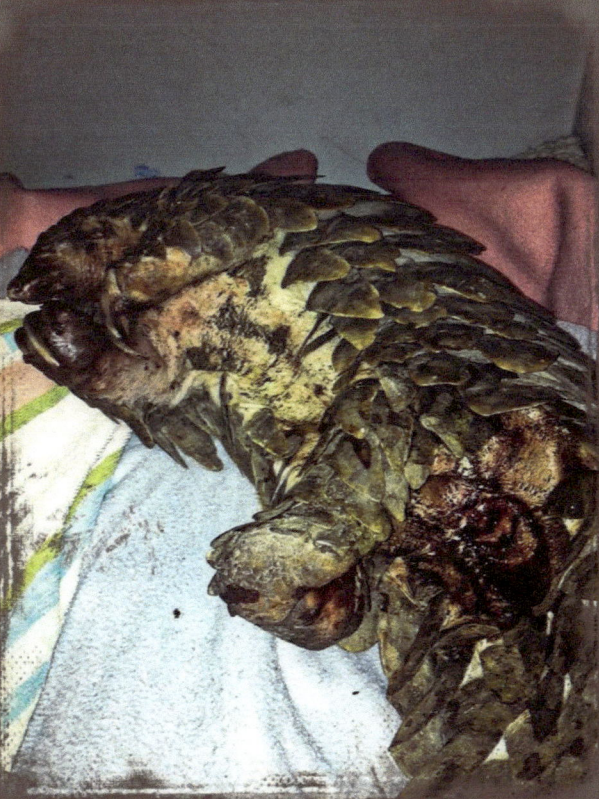
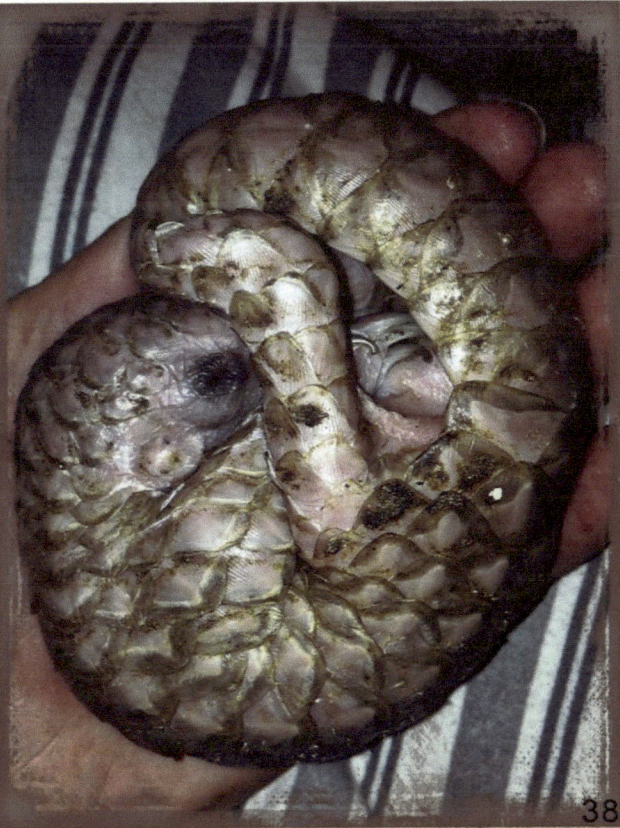

When this adult female was brought in off the black market, she had a red ribbon attached to her based on a belief that it provided protection, which we often saw when the animals came from Chinese sources. She was very scared and underweight, so the decision was made to keep her temporarily since she began to forage for herself in the wild and was allowing us to follow and monitor her. As she gained weight, I considered that if she were pregnant, now would be a horrible time for her to try to find a new territory in the wild, so we held off the release. But by mid-November, she had not given birth, and I started to doubt my belief she was pregnant. I made an appointment with our vet for X-rays as no one had a sonar available.

After taking them, he stared for quite a while and told me I had completely misjudged and that she was not pregnant! He explained that in the X-rays of more common mammals, one sees the fetuses' bone structure clearly, and we assumed that a pangolin would be just as easy to recognize. Years later, a vet shared the X-ray of a pup still in utero, and it was clear to see, but apparently this was also just before delivery. Only recently, after many discussions with specialist pangolin vet Dr. Kelsey Skinner and pangolin conservationist Francois Meyer, have we begun to piece together our various experiences and start asking the less explored questions around pangolin pregnancies.

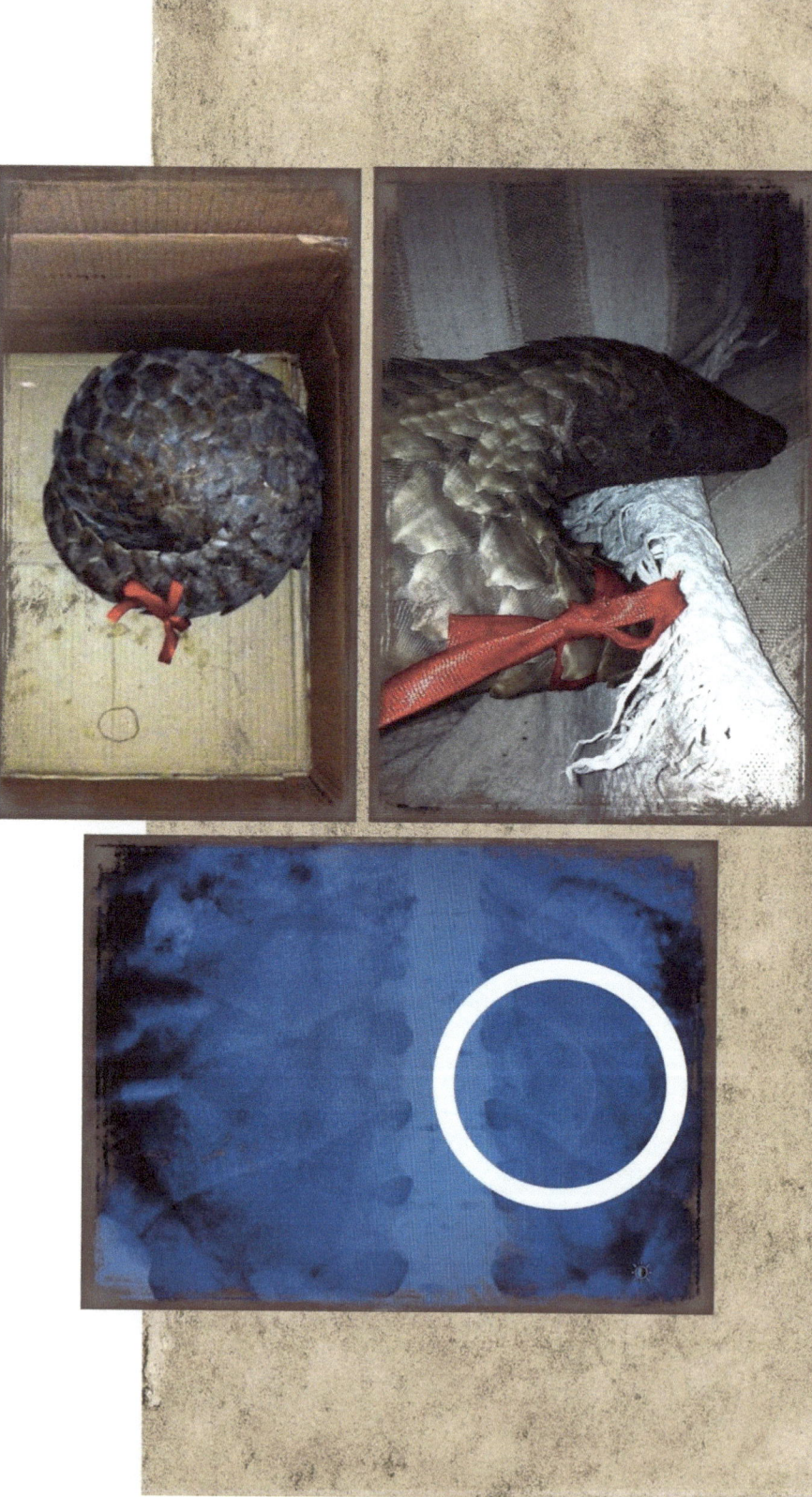

Questions like:
Do pangolins have the ability to regulate their pregnancies through:

1. Halting early embryo development?
2. Terminating and reabsorbing fetuses during very early fetal development?
3. Early stage abortion?
4. Normal gestation (possibly between 6-9 months)
5. Extend their gestation (over at least 8 months)

Through various diagnostic imaging approaches, including radiography, computed tomography (CT), and ultrasound scanning, Dr. Skinner has noted fetal movements during pregnancy that correlate to a theory I have long had on this topic—that the fetus moves position during the course of pregnancy. Starting on the right-hand side of the abdomen, it then crosses the midline (in a more horizontal orientation), and finally positions on the left-hand side of the abdomen before birth.

I was recently asked by a Namibian vet to advise on the case of a wild pangolin that needed urgent care. They believed he was a male, but, in fact, it was a female, and since it was an adult and within my gestation timeline, I asked them to take specific X-rays to look for a fetus.

What we found on June 5, 2020, was definitely the backbone of a tiny fetus in utero. Even if this mama had her pup early in September, it meant this gestation was already definitely three months old, and likely she would only birth in October, which makes it at least four. Factor in that most mammals only show fetal bone structure in the last months of pregnancy, and we probably have a fetus of at least six months-and maybe the unconfirmed nine months that both Roxy and I suspect. However, several questions remain:

1. At what point does the bone structure develop in utero?

2. What are the various internal areas where the mother will carry her pup during different stages of pregnancy, and do these change throughout the pregnancy?

3. Why did we not see a pup during our first X-ray? (Unfortunately, the original X-rays were lost when the clinic was sold, but I still hope that someday they will be discovered and we can reanalyse them.)

Nowadays, it is much more reliable to use a sonar machine, and I have been informed that the heartbeat shows and is easy to recognize. But recently it seems the medical field has raised some health concerns for fetus recognition with sonar machines, so this should not be done often. Back to our patient, I couldn't believe I had been wrong, and I felt incredibly guilty I had held her for a few extra weeks. So I went home and started preparing the vehicle and crate for her release.

The next evening, one of my staff members came running to my house with the news that as he went to take her out for her final monitored bush walk, he realized she had just given birth. In his panic, he had handled the baby accidentally and then just put them both on the ground and ran to me. We madly dashed back to her, but I could immediately see she was rejecting the baby. It was being dragged through the dirt, still attached by the umbilical cord, in her effort to come to me.

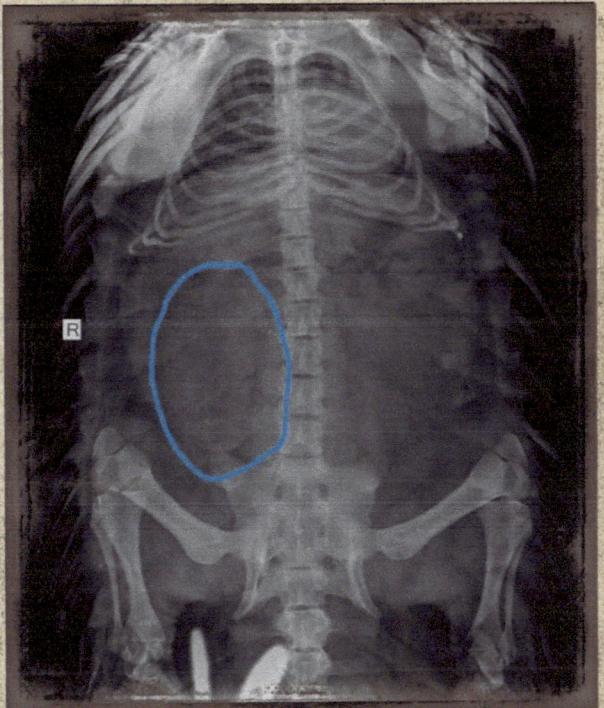

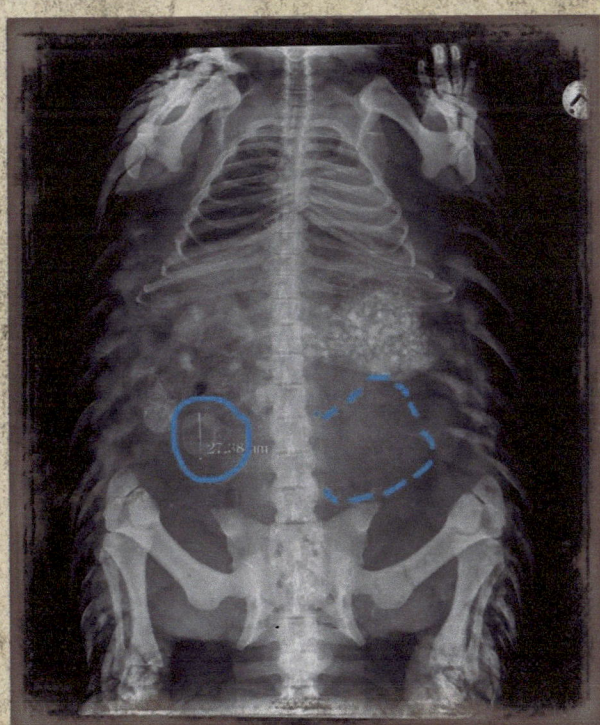

It was horrifying to watch, so I picked them both up, wiped what dirt I could off the baby, and held them together in my arms, hoping she would calm and start to bond. Instead, she continued to want to get closer to me and farther away from her baby.

Perhaps I should have done something differently under the circumstances. Perhaps my staff's early contact caused problems. Perhaps if I had confirmed she was pregnant and been with her during the birth, there would have been a happy ending. Instead, I left staff with mama and I rushed the pup back to my home for warmth and baby pang milk formula He survived only hours and then seemed to decide that life just wasn't worth the effort. Even afterward, the vet said he could not see a baby pangolin pup fetus in those X-rays.

Just over a year later, another mama pang came in off the black market with a pup about six weeks old, still riding on her mother's back and suckling milk. She arrived on December 13, 2015, very abused and weak and the most terrified pangolin I have ever worked with.

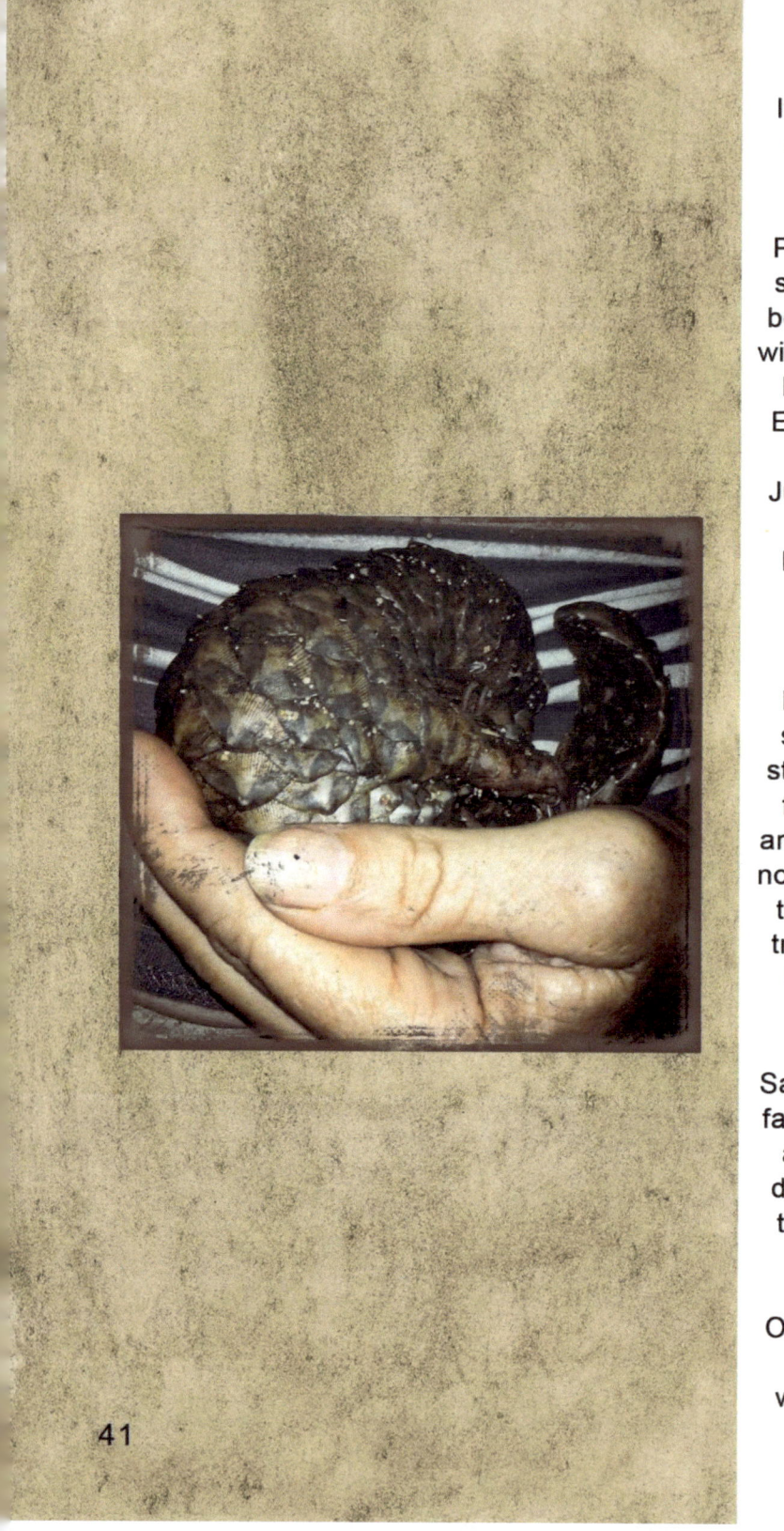

I had received a call three days earlier from a man wishing to sell the mother for N$60,000.00 ($3,800 USD) and the pup for N$20,000.00 ($1,300 USD). This is a large sum of money in any currency, and REST has a strict policy not to pay high fees as we strongly believe this leads the public to go out and capture more pangolins. I spent many frustrating hours negotiating on the telephone. My tactics ranged from sweet to severe and outlining the penalties of being caught in possession of the pangolins. This caller was not an animal trafficker by trade, but a general farm worker who happened to come across the pangolin family and thought he could make some quick money. What most pangolin traffickers do not realize is they are not going to get anything near the prices reported in the papers and paid for in Asia, and—at least in many countries—there is a very good chance they will get caught and put in jail.

Sadly, by the time I had negotiated the pair's release it was due mainly to the fact that the farm workers could see the mother was slowly dying. Mama pang had not eaten for days, all the while still feeding her little pup curled and protected inside her rounded armor. I drove ten hours to a remote location and back and forth on a deserted dirt road until the traders believed I had not brought the police. They finally gave me possession of these poor pangolins, tied up in an old corn sack.

Once on our property, no matter what I did or how far away I followed her, the mother we named Charlize never relaxed enough to eat properly. She would carry her pup for a while, but when she fell off, the mama would often leave the pup, knowing she was just too weak to carry on with the extra weight.

After administering a drip for fluids, we finally made the decision to release Charlize with a tracker until she was strong enough to carry her baby again. Our hope was to discover how long a pup stays with its mother in the wild. We devised a plan to bring the two together daily for bonding while allowing the mother some peace to forage alone. We fitted a radio tracker, but presumably she walked out of range of the VHF (old antenna equipment). Despite aerial and vehicle searches to get a signal, she was never found. Knowing what we do now about releasing pangolins in severe stress, I am almost sure she did not survive.

This is how my beloved Honey Bun pup came into my care. Since that fateful day, many have asked me how I came up with the name Honey Bun. I do not always name the animals in our care (Katiti was named by a lovely young Namibian in a naming contest), but Honey Bun is named after someone very special to REST. Harald Bartsch is a well-known Namibian businessman who happened to visit REST one day, and his love of all animals prompted him to give us a donation. At many difficult moments, Harald always came to REST's aid, and after developing a strong friendship, I decided the next pangolin we received would be named in his honor. How could I have known that a little female pup would soon arrive? After days of thinking of names with the initials HB, a very special friend found a silly song about being someone's "sugar plum, honey bun." Since this little creature was so sweet and loving, the name was perfect. I could never have imagined then that she would become a star and icon for her species.

Raising Honey Bun was another adventure. Since this was my second baby to raise from a very early age, I was able to start noticing "trends." For instance, I realized the pups are first introduced to ants by riding very close to the mother's head. Only older pups ride this far up, and I believe it is so they can be introduced to solid food and possibly start building immunities to formic acid or any other natural toxins the prey produces. As the ants swarm around the mother's head, the baby is stimulated by the mother's licking and starts to lick up stray ants.

When I was having difficulty getting Honey Bun to eat, I took her out on my shoulders, pretended to lick up ants near the ground, and, unbelievably, she took her first ants as food. Whether my theory was right and stimulated her appetite, I do not know, but I do know it worked, so I was happy, even if I am sure I looked absolutely ridiculous.

In 2019, I delayed the release of this book as I was sure Honey Bun was pregnant. I had recorded almost daily instances of mating between her and a large non-releasable male pangolin that had come into the center with a severe leg injury. Amos and Honey Bun had an incredibly close bond and during the mating season would often sleep curled up next to or around each other.

As I mentioned before, no one is sure of the pregnancy length of a pangolin, but we began mentally preparing for an impending birth. Not having all the necessary equipment at our center, I took Honey Bun to a local vet for X-rays and sonar, but I realized the stress was too much for her so decided rather to just wait and see.

Unfortunately, at the time our long-term vet relocated to another country, which meant house calls were not possible. To add to the problems, our area experienced a severe drought. Initially, I was not too worried about the drought as we had enough bush and grass for most wild animals, but what I soon realized was that droughts severely affect ants and termites. Pangolins in Namibia were in for a very problematic year.

44

Observations as I know them

- A newborn pangolin is called a pup, but I have not been able to find out the source of how this name was given.

- As mentioned earlier, there is a definite birthing season in Namibia between October and November. Severe drought seems to delay births until December.

- The mothers show no obvious physical signs of impending birth.

- Gestation may be between six to nine months, but I think it is closer to nine.

- Full-term baby pangolins weigh 300-330 grams at birth.

- Because pangolins are mammals, they give birth to a live pup, which is born yearly or every two years.

- The mother's milk usually comes within twenty-four hours after birth, but the baby appears to suckle before any milk is observed in the mammary glands.

- Just before or at the time of possible conception, Honey Bun's appetite and weight gain increased significantly (as if to boost the coming pregnancy).

- A pup rides on the back of its mother, just behind the head area and over the front shoulders. He can ride nose to tail, or like his mother, or sideways, especially as he gets bigger. They do not ride on the tails of their mothers as tree pangolins do and as is so often reported. Anyone who has watched a ground pangolin walk for any amount of time can easily deduce this as they are perfectly balanced to carry weight on their hind legs, so the extra weight of a baby must be carried closer to the front shoulders.

- A pup stays with its mother for at least three to four months and maybe longer at night. After four months of age, no one has recorded a pup still riding or foraging with its mother, so it was assumed they separate permanently. I believe they may continue to sleep together at night.

• Many believe pangolins are solitary animals once a pup is weaned. I have found that when in captivity, they often sleep together if they are not both mature females or both mature males. During what I believe is a mating season, a pair will sleep together after an hour or two of mating. Pups going through rehabilitation, even if not related, will often bond with one of the adult pangolins permanently in our care. We expected this would be with the adult female, but I observed a few bonding with our adult male. Of course, when wild ones are sighted during foraging, they will be alone as the ants form formic acid so no two older pangolins can eat together. This does not mean they sleep alone. I once found three dead pangolins along an electric fence within a four-meter radius. They were an adult, a juvenile, and a youngster. We still need to test for genetics, but these samples could help answer the question of family units. Were these dead pangolins related and somehow either died together or died one after another while searching for family members, or were their deaths in the same area just a coincidence? I have also heard a secondhand report of a juvenile pangolin found alive near the site of its presumed mother, who had died due to electric fencing. In addition, Francois Meyer has observed in his camera trap research how a released female from the black market left her pup in the den with a male who it appeared had become her mate but could not have been the pup's father as she was introduced to the area already pregnant. The male stayed with the pup and seemed to accept it by showing no aggression. Pangolins in captivity will usually accept each other if:

1. They are of different sexes at any age,
2. Both young of any sex,
3. One immature and one adult of any sex.

• In the past, young pangolins between the ages of three to nine months that came into REST for rehabilitation had a lower chance of survival than adults. During one drought, 90% of our rescues were in this age group, and many had been found searching for food in populated areas. I believe this was due to desperation and inexperience. Most experts believe that a youngster should not be released until at least over a year old or 3 kg. One theory is that the parents pushed them out of their territory early as there simply was not enough food for all of them. From casual conversations with my colleagues in other southern African countries, Namibian pangolin weights seem to be generally much lower and they increase weight slower than our wetter and more fertile neighboring habitats do, so REST tends to keep a pup a bit longer to increase its weight to at least 4 kg. During that fateful year of so many youngsters, they all began successful supervised foraging in the wild, gained weight, grew confident around their handler, and seemed to be thriving. This continued for weeks and sometimes months until one day they became lethargic, no longer wanted to eat, and despite antibiotics and rehydration, often died within days. The postmortem of one such pup found his stomach filled with pebbles but no food. Outside observation appeared to show he was eating, gaining weight, and healthy, but this proves that was not sufficient evidence of health. Questions like these remain by far the most frustrating and devastating aspects of my work, and right or wrong, I lose a piece of my heart with each death. I believe our newest rehabilitation protocols will help determine deficiencies through blood analysis much earlier and thus help us to provide extra nutrients through temporary tube feeding, but this does not solve the unknown root of the problem that often occurs during droughts.

"

Maturity and longevity

No one knows how long pangolins live, but most researchers in Africa will guess anything between eight to fifteen years. I personally believe at least fifteen and maybe longer.

In Japan at the Ueno Zoo, a Chinese pangolin is believed to be the longest held pangolin in any captive situation at twenty-three years, while in Africa records show a ground pangolin named Marimba has been held for thirteen years. At REST, the longest we held a pangolin was Honey Bun, who was with us for four years, six months, and twenty-two days, except for two periods in her life when she was on her own for days or weeks in the wild. Our first baby, Katiti, was held for three years, one month, and nineteen days before his auto release, which essentially means that reintroduction did not go as planned. Katiti's return to the wild is one of those stories in which everything that could have gone wrong did.

When Roxy and Katiti first came in, I had just divorced. As I was looking for some land to make a home for REST, a local lodge owner approached me while our sons played rugby together. The next day I was invited to visit the newly bought reserve, and we discussed future plans for establishing a leading conservation area. Sadly, the relationship began to disintegrate as the owners made a financial decision to focus more on hunting than conservation. Water supply was cut, eviction notice was given, attorneys were hired, and I finally admitted that a small financial settlement was the best I was going to get because if I continued, I would probably lose everything, including my sanity.

I moved off the property and had just started raising Honey Bun while a long-term staff member oversaw Katiti on the old farm. We were still deciding whether it would be best to bring him to the new area or release him in the habitat he had grown up in. While staying seemed best for his physical and mental welfare, I was concerned about his safety if we were no longer in the area to monitor him.

On the new site, I was building basic structures as fast and as cheaply as I could on a portion of land that a farmer along the Etosha National Park had promised he could get a waiver for and sell to me. Namibian law requires that the government must give permission for the sale of any farmland. Because this was an area of only 300 ha (roughly 740 acres), I assumed the landowner was well-informed that this would be possible, and to be quite honest, I was desperate to make a home for REST. Katiti's walker was supposed to check his tracker signal every day before walking to ensure the battery of the unit was still functioning. It is something that every student and staff member at REST learns the first week. I'd visited the old farm four days previously while packing a moving truck and had personally tested the unit then. Later in the week, she called to say she had lost him in the shadows of sunset, and as it was late, she would track him the next day. I insisted she do it that night to get a direction of his movement, and she informed me later there was no signal.

After rushing to the site, I discovered the entire week she had simply overlooked checking the signal, the transmitter battery had died, and Katiti was gone. I was absolutely devastated. It was Christmastime, so she went on holiday. I had to focus on raising baby Honey Bun, and my strong, brave Katiti went wild without me being able to monitor his welfare.

I hired my son and some friends to search intensively, and we found tracks, but Katiti continued to elude us for a tracker refitting. Eventually, I decided this was his territory, he knew it well, and in a world that is seldom ideal, it was time to let go. REST left the property, but I knew in my heart and mind that we had prepared him for life on his own. The area was where he had been born and grew up, so to move him would have been a disservice to all the years spent preparing him for the wild. But I still regretted that, once again, due to events beyond my control, a pangolin I loved was in the wild without having the ability to track its safety. Katiti had taught me so much about pangolins and allowed me insight and the ability to share my experience with others through writing and photographs. Wherever he went, I went, and it was quite an adventure. He was amazing, and I know in my heart, he still roams this earth.

Just how long a pangolin lives can only be guessed at. It is often assumed that animals in captivity live longer than their counterparts in the wild, but my instinct tells me that with pangolins this may be false for the following reasons.

- I believe stress plays an extremely important role in the survival rate of pangolins. We are working on a theory that once a capture takes place, the stress levels increase to such an extent that reducing them becomes difficult. This stress often leads to death with symptoms of pneumonia. Many assume pneumonia is the cause, but I believe it is the result. The easiest way to explain this is by looking at the relationship between HIV/AIDS and pneumonia. Often pneumonia is listed as the cause of death, but it is a symptom of the HIV virus. Dr. Karin Lourens was the first to suggest to me that the lungs are the "shock" organ of a pangolin, and in my opinion, there is no doubt she is right. Most pangolin postmortems show severe lung damage, and lack of this damage became a key element in two future pangolin deaths that would dramatically change my life once again.

- Pangolins are one of the oldest creatures alive today. They have survived drought, floods, disease, and predators. It is hard to argue that a captive situation could be better suited for a longer life. But everything taken into consideration leads me to believe that pangolins will often, if not always, do better in the wild than in captivity, except for cases in which they are too small, weak, or injured to survive on their own.

- Some colleagues believe young pangolins often forage during daylight hours to avoid the large nocturnal predators. While this may be true, I witnessed very few differences between young and old pangolins in my care and believe that most pangolins walk during daylight hours more than previously documented.

- It is reported that an adult pangolin can emit a very strong odor from its anal gland as defence, but I have never had a pangolin do so.

How to age a pangolin

Having handled several pangolins of various ages, I believe I can correctly identify a pangolin through the first four years of its life based on the size, shape, color, and texture of its scales and afterward from ages between five to eight and more than nine years old. As I mentioned before, I believe Namibian pangolins are quite a bit leaner than other African countries, and all of the babies I raised were taken to forage naturally at the same time they would have gone wild with their birth mothers, so we never experienced overweight babies still on unnatural milk for extended periods. The first four years are easy and can be determined as follows.

- Birth to 1 year - the scales are dark in color with light stripes running down the middle from top to bottom. I believe this is a form of camouflage. Each scale also has a sharp point at the end of the scale, which I believe gives it an extra defence against predators. The scale surface is smooth.
+-300 g at birth.

- 1-2 years old - the stripes are just growing out to the last quarter at the end of the scales. Most tips are less pointy but retain some small points in the center back area and tail base. The scales are starting to become rippled like a seashell where they are growing out from the base of the skin.

- 2-3 years old - all the white stripes have grown out and there are few if any pointy tips at the ends of the scales. The scales may have a small area at the tip of the scale that is still smooth, but most of the scale is textured with ridges and is of medium size.

• 4 years old - the scales look basically the same as the year before but with little or nothing left of the earlier smooth areas on the scale tip. The scales are growing much wider as the animal gains weight.

5-8 years old – this is determined by the size of the scale. The rippled shell effect is still consistent throughout the entire scale.

• Over 8 years old – about 1/3 - 1/2 of the scale from the tip up starts to become smooth. I believe this is a result of the scale growth slowing down, probably due to age and nutrition, and could happen earlier in areas where the ground they roll into every night is rough or sandy, thus acting like sandpaper to smooth the scale surface.

Unfortunately, as I was preparing this book, an individual in the Namibian government decided to confiscate 21 years' worth of frozen animals samples and all of the legally taxidermied pangolin specimens that I have always used for education. After repeatedly asking for their return or at least access to measure, count, and weigh them, I am having to publish without this vital data of exact scale size measurements.

"

Are pangolins vocal?

Most published information and field researchers will tell you that pangolins make no vocalization, but this is incorrect. Only someone who has spent considerable time with a pangolin that is not afraid will know they make a variety of sniffing noises that have various meanings depending on the tone, volume, and circumstances surrounding the noise.

Until quite recently, there were only two occasions I heard a pangolin make what I can only call a whelping cry. The first time was when baby Katiti was pinched while curled up inside his mother. I heard it only once, observed his struggling, and then because I never heard it again assumed I had imagined it. You cannot believe my surprise when five years later I had an injured pangolin at the vet—who had been shot and we were trying to see if we could determine the trajectory of the bullet—when the vet turned to me and asked if I could hear as my poor pangolin, called Skater Boy, moaned in pain for about twenty seconds.

In late 2019, Honey Bun also made some barely audible whelping sighs. When I comforted her with soft words and rubbed her tummy or back, she immediately settled and usually slept. Little did I know then that Honey Bun was actually very sick and those moments would haunt me for the rest of my life.

Pangolins will also reflect their feelings through behavior. A quick slashing back and forth of the tail is a sure sign of displeasure and defence, and the sharp-edged scales can cut humans or animals easily and deeply. A pangolin relaxed around a human will approach them and curiously climb over and around them. Most of the infants I have raised loved licking my hair, possibly bonding with me as pangolins will often lick between each others' scales.

Observations as I know them

- When they wake and when they go to sleep, ground pangolins make a short, single sniffing noise that sounds very much like a small sneeze to another pangolin or person they trust. If they receive a similar response, they may repeat the back and forth vocalization up to three times. They visually relax during and after this ceremony. This sniffing back and forth can also take place when the pangolin smells a new person or finds itself in a situation in which it requires a little reassurance.

- A strong, continuing, longer sniff takes place when one pangolin is demonstrating they dominate another. It sounds like they are blowing bursts of air out of their nose and lasts up to two seconds. The older pangolin is usually the dominate, regardless of whether male or female. The only time I have seen a younger pangolin dominate an older one is if the youngster has been hand raised and is responding to an incoming pangolin, thus showing it feels secure in its territory.

- Another form of dominance is best described as vibrating their entire body. They rattle their scales, and I have seen and heard similar behavior in porcupine when they are unsettled.

- The whelping cry is short and high-pitched and can be a single, short whelp, which I suspect indicates a sharp pain that subsides, or the longer one after another in short succession, like moans of severe pain.

- A very soft, almost continuous moan is done by a pangolin that is in discomfort and wishes to get some reassurance. I have only ever heard this vocalization from Honey Bun.

"

What kills pangolins?

Visitors often ask me what kills a pangolin. In all honestly, their main threat is man. As the Asian species of pangolins were hunted to the brink of extinction, black-market mafias dealing with everything from rhino to human trafficking began sourcing existing pangolin scales from animals that had been killed years before in the bush meat trade in central and west Africa.

Consumer demand increased, and as the stocks dwindled, the only alternative source for the growing demand was to capture, kill, and smuggle live pangolins. This probably began in the more remote areas of central, west, and east Africa, but as profits rose so did the trade in southern Africa.

In Namibia, the environment in which pangolins are found is usually relatively wild, wide-open spaces. These vast tracts of land allow poaching to occur as sheer land size makes monitoring difficult. Historically, overgrazing of cattle has allowed much of the ranch land to become overgrown with thick, thorny bush. There is a recent trend in our area to eliminate bush with unskilled labor, and various methods have been quite effective and poverty alleviation is argued. Unfortunately, supervision of duties is often only monitored at the end of each day or week by the amount of cut bush lying on the ground. If only a small percentage of this labor force checks and possibly digs out every burrow they come across during the hottest parts of the day, then a large percentage of pangolins and similar animals, such as aardvarks and warthogs, will be found and potentially captured or killed. Traditional methods of detection and tracking of the perpetrators is not possible as the smugglers are legally on the land, their crime is difficult to monitor, and the animal parts are small and easy to hide.

Dead pangolin scales can be transported in either small or large containers, are not easily crushed, and elements like water do not destroy them in transit. Rhino and elephant are easier to monitor with tracking on foot, by vehicle, or from the air, and smaller animals, such as birds and amphibians, are easier to hold in shipping cages and containers and do not experience the severe symptoms of stress that cause so many pangolin deaths. These smaller species are also often given better care as their value is usually much higher when alive, while both scale collection and meat consumption is not contingent on a pangolin being alive.

Occasionally honey badger, one of the strongest and most fearless creatures alive, will manage to pry a pangolin open and kill it, and less occasionally a hyena will manage a kill, with some of the strongest jaws of any animal in Africa, but observers have photographed and videoed leopard, lion, and other large predators trying to kill pangolins without success. The pangolin simply rolls up in a protected armored ball, and the predator eventually gives up and leaves, at which time the pangolin unrolls and walks away completely unharmed. Very few people in the world will ever see an unrolled, relaxed pangolin, but if the pangolins have complete trust, they will pee on themselves as a cooling mechanism when warm and then lie completely exposed.

Man-made developments can unintentionally kill pangolins, either through lack of awareness or lack of finding pangolin-compatible solutions to their fencing problems. The most well-known man-made threat is electrical fences as many farms in southern Africa have installed electrical wires to keep out poachers and predators and to keep other species confined within their boundaries. The lowest wires are considered essential for warthog that love to dig under fences and create perfect escape routes for many other species.

Unfortunately, when a pangolin touches the lower wire and receives a shock, it tends to defensively roll up and often accidentally rolls around the wire. Even if the shock is on pulse, every time it starts to relax another shock occurs, and it wraps its body around the wire tighter, not knowing it will soon cause its own death. I have found a few pangolins that appeared to be electrocuted and have moved slightly away from the fence—so they may not have rolled around the wire—but have either died from the initial electrification or been so dazed that a passing predator was able to kill them while unrolled and still in shock.

I once had a pangolin in my care that died of poison. A friend and I had each taken a pangolin to forage within visuals of each other but in separate areas. He was with Honey Bun, and I had a new young male. Neither would eat, so we switched animals. Honey Bun moved slightly down the border and continued to refuse to eat, but I remember congratulating my friend on managing to get the little boy to eat. Within twelve hours, the little boy pangolin was dead, and my friend never got over his regret, even though it had nothing to do with the two of us.

We were never able to prove the use of poison, but I found out later that others in the area knew many stories about this farmer on the border of Etosha National Park baiting and killing lions with poison simply for their skins. I am usually an incredibly forgiving person, but to this day I simply cannot forgive the intentional actions of this individual—for not only baiting lions that had caused him and his cattle no harm, but also for allowing me to walk my pangolins in an area he knew was deadly. I moved out of that area soon afterward, and while it hurt us financially, it was my only ethical option.

• The distribution of pangolin scales in Asia has occurred for centuries. I prefer to call their use "traditional belief" rather than "traditional medicine" for the simple fact that the chemical composite of a pangolin scale is 100% the same as a human fingernail. They also grow, wear down, break, and can be injured at the base like a fingernail. A quick internet search will show pangolin scales have been reported to be effective in curing lactation problems for women, erectile problems in men, excessive nervousness, hysterical crying in children, malarial fever, deafness, seizures, poverty, women possessed by the devil (note only women were referred to as beneficiaries), and to ward away ogres (yes, like Shrek!). None of these claims has any documented evidence, but there has been at least one study that reported consumed pangolin scales as potentially harmful to the human system.

• Around 2014, the demand for scales increased drastically. There are two preferred theories as to why. Firstly, the availability of rhino horn became harder to access, and due to the rarity of pangolin scales, they were instantly more valuable. Secondly, a high-ranking Chinese government official diagnosed with cancer went into remission and publicly stated that his "cure" was due to the use of pangolin scales in his treatment.

• Asia, and particularly China, have strong cultural beliefs that require hosts to provide the highest level of hospitality to their guests. This is often interpreted that a good host will serve exotic and expensive food items, making pangolin meat a valuable commodity. As recently as 2015, the government served pangolin meat at State dinners.

• In 2007, China legislated a ban on the hunting of pangolins, in 2018 a ban on importing them, and in 2020 scales were banned in traditional medicine, but historical stocks are still legally used for the treatment of cancer in China, and this allows the viability of continued trade as it is hard to determine the difference between pre-existing and new stocks.

• In the past few years, I received reports that social media in Asia was circulating information that pangolin scales are shed and regrow naturally. Upon further investigation, it appears this information may have been distributed by the illegal traffickers themselves because of the public's increasing interest in protecting pangolin. They hoped that if they could convince the public that pangolin scales were collected without harm to the animal, use would continue. The fact is there is no way to remove a pangolin scale fully or partially from the body of the animal without causing life-threatening damage.

- Many African cultures value pangolin meat for similar reasons. Its rarity gives it value. Traditional law often requires that if someone from the tribe finds a pangolin, they are required to take it to their traditional leader or, as in the country of Zimbabwe, to the president. Beliefs in the local Namibian Herero tribe require that a pangolin be taken to the chief, who traditionally throws it into the fire alive. Once cooked, the meat is distributed and is believed to bring good luck to all who eat it. REST has worked closely with traditional leaders and found that if we can fund visits to the center, traditional and community leaders become so enamored with the pangolins they are introduced to that they are willing to adjust their beliefs to fit into modern times. One method allows the chiefs and respected members of the community to a have a photo taken with a live pangolin.

This has only been done with pangolins we had raised and that were not stressed if we were around. Initially, we allowed them to hold the pangolin for a moment, but we have since decided they can only stand nearby. We have them wash their hands, remain quiet, and stand still—all in the interest of the pangolin. The physical photo they take home becomes a valuable commodity and is believed to hold more power than just a bite of meat. In return for their newfound respect of pangolins, the chief tells the community that everyone must leave wild pangolins in peace so as not to disturb the powerful gifts that the picture provides. These declarations are coming from within the leadership of the communities themselves and thus hold much more authority than from me, other organizations, or even national laws.

- Pangolins can get parasites, and at least one well-known tree pangolin was reported to have died from a newly discovered one, but most I have observed were either ticks acquired from domestic dog areas while held captive by poachers or natural flea-type parasites found in wild warthog or aardvark burrows.

"

Pangolin diet

I believe that tree pangolin species adapt much better to a captive environment if the holding facility is equipped for both their mental and physical needs. Asia has some very important advantages with food supply as ant larvae are easily available for purchase and they have access to tree-dwelling ant nests that, if managed sustainably, provide a safe, easy, and affordable diet.

Ground pangolins, however, do not generally survive in long-term captivity, and a large part of this is due to diet. I am often asked what the pangolins in our care eat, and the simple answer is most of them refuse to eat any form of captive diet. Some do accept various items, but we have never discovered an artificial diet that all or even most pangolins will accept. A few eat this and a few eat that, and they remain alive, but are they healthy, and are we really providing everything their unique systems need?

For instance, pangolins consume small pebbles and dirt when eating, and these circulate in the stomach, grinding up the ants and termites for easier digestion. If a captive diet does not technically require this digestive method, one must decide if the pebbles and soil are still required, could they perform a less obvious function, and if needed, how to source and supply the proper quality and quantity.

It is possible to determine if there are pangolins on a property by looking at their feeding sites. These are small diggings in the ground, and a pangolin's is almost always triangular in shape as its claws dig from a center spot to each side. An aardvark, on the other hand, has much larger feet with stronger claws and digs from front to back, so the diggings are more rounded and one can often see the individual claw scratchings still in the sides of the soil. Similar yet smaller, rounded diggings are done by aardwolf.

REST's success in raising and rehabilitating pangolins for the wild is because we have dedicated men and women whose sole job is to take pangolins out into the wild bush every day and follow behind them for hours while they forage naturally. This not only provides the best diet, but allows them normal exercise and mental stimulation. These walkers are the true heroes of REST. While this seems like a dream job, it requires qualities not easy to find. First and foremost, they must bond with their pangolins, and if they do not have this ability, then nothing else matters.

They must have infinite patience with new pangolins that have only experienced humans at their worst. These pangolins will sometimes hide under bushes-leaving the walker to stand for hours in the heat-swish their tails in aggression, or wiggle and claw when picked up. It usually takes hours and sometimes days for them to slowly build up trust and respect.

Pangolin dig

Pangolin dig

Aardvark dig

64

- They work varied and odd hours as our pangolins wake naturally, so they must always be on standby.

• They must be aware of security from predators, snakes, and humans. For obvious reasons, we do not freely share our security protocols, but there are many, and all pangolins and their keepers are continually monitored.

- A walker and assistant also take out iPads with programs that allow them to record every movement made by the pangolin—when and where they walk, when they rest, sleep or burrow in a hole, what they eat, when, and how often. If they use the toilet, it is noted, and the feces is collected to test for content, hormones, and parasites. In other words, every action is documented for research and has advanced our knowledge considerably.

• Namibia can be a harsh and unforgiving land. It is hot, dry, full of thorny bush, sometimes rocky and mountainous, and is very isolated. It is not an easy job to do day after day—come rain or shine, holiday or sickness. Regardless of these challenges, a captive pangolin must be walked daily, and our staff is dedicated to this mission.

Very rarely, a captive pangolin will accept an artificial diet. I don't consider this healthy long-term, but it is beneficial for short-term recovery. This was the case with one very special large male pangolin we named Amos.

The day began before sunrise when I was called by nature conservation officials who had worked through the night. A pangolin had been found in the industrial area of a town, and I was asked to fetch him and give a veterinary check. He came into our care with all expectations of an early release, but the moment I put him on the ground, I could see he was limping badly on his back left foot.

His rescuer and I discussed a theory as to what had probably happened. We believe he was caught in the wild from a cattle farming area (due to the manure under his scales) and kept in captivity for at least a few days on a hard cement floor (due to scratches on his scales). He was then taken to town to be sold on the black market. Industrial buildings often have very small windows for security, and because they are high and tiny, they are left open in our extreme heat. I believe that because pangolins are determined climbers, Amos managed to make his way inside the building to one of these windows. Faced with captivity or escape, he chose to go out the window, not able to determine how high he was, nor how far he would fall. Hitting the ground at such a distance broke his middle back scale to the base.

Pangolin feces

X-rays were taken showing a total femoral spinal fracture. This basically meant the left back leg bone was completely severed from his spine. It is not an uncommon procedure to fix on many animals. However, due to a pangolin's outside armor, the only way to operate is to access the injury from the soft stomach area, which is a procedure—to my knowledge—that has never been attempted on any pangolin species.

The consulting vets felt the best available option was to not operate and hope for the best, but they gave him little chance of survival. They insisted I limit his movement to give the break some time to heal, but they had no idea what a difficult task they were asking. How could I get him to eat if he wasn't supposed to move?

We sought advice from expert colleagues, and Lisa Hywood of the Tikki Hywood Foundation (THF) in Zimbabwe suggested we carry him to ant areas and manually dig for him so he could feed without much movement. This method had been very successful for some of THF's more difficult cases but was a complete disaster with Amos as he still didn't trust us. He began losing weight so fast that I knew he would soon be weak and die before I could get him to forage.

With the help of Lisa, a local vet and I performed our first sedation of a pangolin, and I can tell you it was as scary as first things often are. I have immense respect for vets who are willing to perform procedures they have never been trained for, and this happens quite often as pangolin protocols are still being established. After much consideration, the vet and I chose to take the opportunity to tube feed Amos while sedated as he was still terrified of humans and any interaction without sedation was difficult.

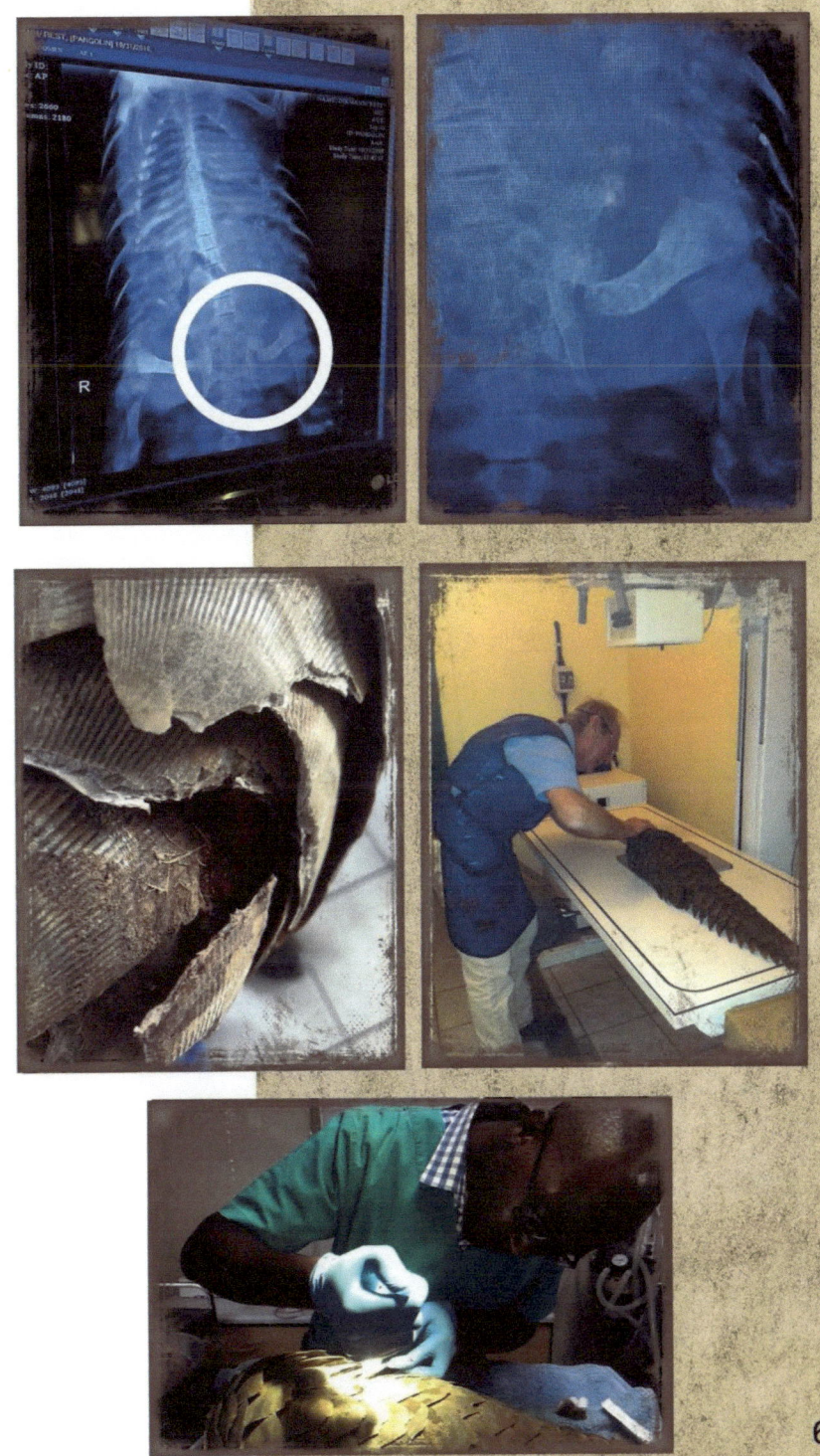

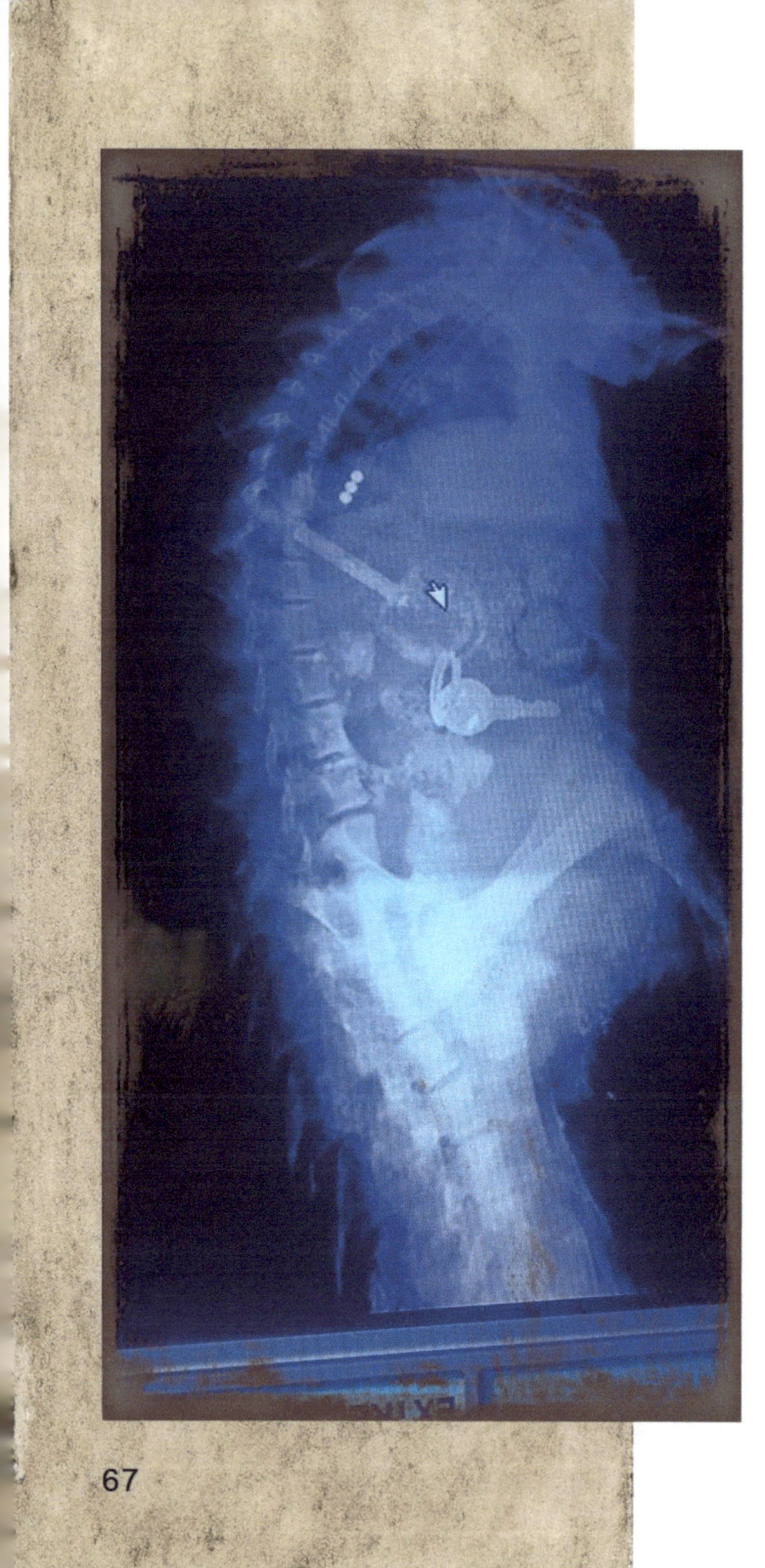

We decided to tube feed him two days in a row as we needed to take X-rays under anesthetic anyway and felt this would boost his energy and digestion, but we knew it was not a procedure we could continue for the minimum six weeks healing time. The vet was located a few hours away, so that meant either the daily stress of long-distance travel or the continuous stress of being held at a clinic not designed for pangolins. And weeks of anesthetic would not be healthy.

At the time, tube feeding was considered a risky procedure, but nowadays I am confident performing it and have even been able to assist vets, in addition to demonstrating methods for collecting blood and putting in IV tubes. Disagreements are still widespread on anesthetic, with some arguing it must be used to minimize stress and others arguing it is safer without. Having personally tube fed with and without anesthetic (in an emergency), I would recommend always sedating a wild pangolin with something safe like isoflurane.

As a side note, one of the oddest events in my life happened with an X-ray machine during this time. The vet and I agreed to take an X-ray to make sure we had correctly inserted the feeding tube (seen with the 3 dots at the end). You simply cannot imagine our surprise when we also saw keys inside Amos's stomach on the X-ray. We carried on with the feeding due to time constraints with the sedation and then stood confounded. It was finally decided to think over the night, and I can still remember driving home going through every possible scenario. Had the poachers hidden keys under his skin? Why hide something valuable in a pangolin they knew was illegally held? Could he have swallowed them? Impossible, as I knew his mouth and throat were too small. By the time I arrived home and inspected Amos carefully for any scars, I only knew that those keys could not possibly be inside him, but I had no explanation for the X-ray. The vet also spent a long night trying to figure out our mystery, and the next day we finally had our solution.

The X-ray machine had required maintenance the day before I brought Amos in. The technician had performed one last test before leaving and had used his personal keys to test the plate. Somehow the plate had not been erased and, coincidentally, we had placed Amos in the exact same spot to overlap the previous key X-ray with his stomach. We still smile about it today, but for a few hours it was a confounding mystery we had no idea how to solve.

In Amos's case, I cannot explain what happened next better than this. I sat with Amos in my arms and talked with him—willing him to eat a captive diet or die. There was nothing else I could do for him, so his will to live had to come from within.

Next, I put a mattress for myself on the floor next to a pangolin-friendly room so that if he chose to, he could easily approach and leave me at will, hoping he would take positive cues from Honey Bun, who also had access to the room. She would come visit me, sniff, nap, etc., and very quickly Amos was waking me throughout the night as he constantly walked around, above, and over me at all hours. He loved having his back gently rubbed as it eased some of the pain, and he soon was eating an always-evolving captive diet. I have tried these same foods with numerous pangolins, and not one of them has eaten much, even when starving.

As Amos began to heal, I had a young man named Ben volunteering with REST who was willing to dedicate himself completely to his care. Amos still had a persistent wound on his back that we treated daily, and unfortunately, due to his limp, he did not have the strength to forage the three to five hours needed for 100% of his dietary needs. However, he was still taken into the bush every day and monitored by his walker so he could forage naturally, go into wild burrows, and essentially get to experience all that a wild pangolin does, while still coming home to get the veterinary treatment he needed for his survival.

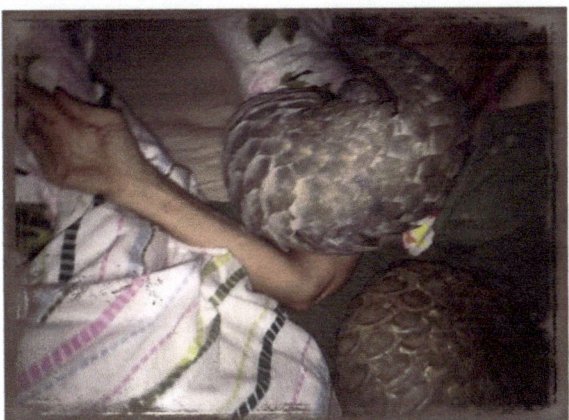

• Ground pangolins prefer ants over termites, generally eating at twenty ant sites for every one termite site. In the rainy season, their favorite food is the ant eggs suspected to be favored as highly nutritious and not containing any toxins. Ant preference occurs unless they are weak or weather conditions, such as drought, have negatively affected ant populations, in which case they will consume more termites than ants for two to five days. I believe this may be due to two main reasons:

1.   Termites have considerably more protein than ants, provide more nutrition faster, and are less aggressive. Namibia has at least forty-two species of termite, but our research on which are preferred is not complete. I believe that individual pangolins have individual preferences, depending on where they have grown up and what food was available.

2.   Ants produce formic acid when under threat from predators. Formic acid is deadly to most species, including humans, and will kill a pangolin that eats too many from one site or visits that site too often. They have been recorded to produce higher doses at a faster rate when disturbed too often. REST discovered during the 2019-2020 severe drought that our property was not big enough to provide food for both the wild pangolin and aardvark that we have in addition to the captive long- and short-term pangolins in our care. Fortunately, our neighbors allowed us to cross borders and utilize their land, and in return we monitored for snares and poachers' tracks.

•   When pangolins eat termites, it is usually the wood termite species. Only four times in the thousands I have personally walked behind a pangolin have I observed them eating harvester termites, so named because they harvest grass. Seasonally, these termites move together in very large numbers and would be an easy and nutritious meal, but pangolins in my care have never liked eating them.

• Pangolins can close their nose and ears when confronted by aggressive ants. During these attacks, they will also develop a thick mucus around their eyes, which is presumed to be some form of protection.

68

- I have heard reports—but do not agree—that pangolins will allow the ants to climb under their scales so they can intentionally crush them and eat them later.

- Ground pangolins forage daily, and if water is accessible will drink daily. It is believed that if water is not available, they can access enough hydration from ants and termites to last for up to two weeks. Those living in very arid areas may supply their body's liquid requirement solely from their food.

- General pangolin weights in Namibia differ quite drastically from other southern African countries, with an average adult Namibian pangolin weighing between 7.5-9 kg (16.5 -19.8 lbs) and a southern African counterpart normally 9-12 kg (19.8-26.5 lbs). I believe these discrepancies are not genetic, but due to richer soils and habitats supporting larger food bases.

- A pangolin's tongue is almost as long as its body, not including the tail area, and reaches up to 40 cm (14 in). It is attached near the pelvis and last pair of ribs and not in the mouth, like most mammals. It curls up and is stored in the chest area when not in use.

- Pangolins have no teeth, but ingest tiny bits of dirt, sand, and pebbles when they stick their tongues into ant and termite holes. Once inside the stomach, these bits of nature grind and help digest the ant and termite bodies.

- Individual pangolins seem to have preferences on where they eat. Some prefer turning stones, others search at tree bases, and many find small holes everywhere. I suspect this preference comes from the environment in which they were born and raised.

• The feces of a pangolin often contain large parts of the ant exoskeleton, which is not digested.

• On average, a ground pangolin swallows every 0.9 seconds. This means the tongue extends almost every second of each minute they are eating. On average, almost all pangolins I observed under normal circumstances eat approximately fifteen minutes out of every hour, and most forage on average for three to five hours daily. If one extrapolates this data, factoring in that on each swallow they only consume a minimum one ant or termite, the minimum average of consumed food would be:

PER DAY = 3,000-5,000 individual ants and/or termites
PER MONTH = 90,000-150,000 individual ants and/or termites
PER YEAR = 1,080,000-1,800,000 individual ants and/or termites.

However, I believe that the number of ants or termites consumed is much more than just one per swallow (based on X-rays of stomach content in wild pangolins needing veterinary care). Assuming at least seven and maybe up to fifteen individuals are consumed on average with each swallow, the numbers increase drastically and would put average total consumption numbers at:

PER DAY = 21,000-75,000 individual ants and/or termites
PER MONTH = 630,000-2,250,000 individual ants and/or termites
PER YEAR = 7,560,000-27,000,000 individual ants and/or termites.

The above is not pure data analysis, but until we do more research, I believe it provides a basis that can help not only understand our wild pangolin's environmental needs but also the amounts needed to feed a captive pangolin in either short- or medium-term care.

"

The next big event

I must admit, I am horrible at keeping secrets. I will ask my staff to keep information confidential regarding a unique observation until researched more, and then the next nice and fascinated guest that visits, all the information just comes pouring out of my mouth. I love sharing my passion with others, so it is hard to keep quiet.

You can only imagine the difficulty I had keeping a very big secret about Honey Bun and not shouting from the rooftops when we thought she was pregnant. The story surrounding her pregnancy is filled with elements of suspense, romance, and mystery novels combined—excitement, drama, heartbreak, separation, reunion, tension, illness, confusion, and finally, death.

I suspected Honey Bun was pregnant long before anyone else. By that time our big non-releasable male Amos had settle in, and the two had formed a very close friendship, often sleeping in the same room by choice or curled up next to each other. I observed what appeared to be mating, discussed in a previous chapter. During this month, Honey Bun and Amos had access and chose to move into a warmer room next to their normal housing. They would sleep together every evening, and Amos was often the first to wake for foraging, while Honey Bun slept much later.

I had learned my lesson years before with Roxy and Katiti, and that year I ordered ten VHF trackers from overseas for the rehabilitation season (not enough, but all REST could afford). VHF trackers are too basic for good research, but they do allow an animal's location to be monitored and are still my preferred method as they are small, light, and do not negatively affect the pangolin in any noticeable way. When the trackers arrived via a visiting guest, I opened the long-anticipated box only to discover the designers had decided, without consultation, to redesign the width of the unit, assuming this would make it more stable, but, in fact, it caused major problems.

The scale just above the base of the tail where we mount the trackers is curved, but the unit itself has a flat bottom. Increasing the width of the unit meant the screws holding the tracker in place now had major gaps between the unit and the scale. This open space made the scale prone to damage or loss of a tracker. I immediately sent the package back to the manufacturers with the same guest and only kept one unit to fit on Honey Bun. Within a few weeks, the new tracker malfunctioned and was removed.

What happened the very next day could not have been made up in my wildest nightmares. That day as I was distracted by a few small crises, including builders, paying bills, and an AWOL staff member, Honey Bun woke early and managed to escape from her sleeping area. Being a determined pangolin, she climbed a wall and went over a door. About an hour later, when I realized what had happened, it was all-hands-on-deck, and everyone was given a direction to walk in the hope that someone would see her.

As her missing days progressed, I cannot describe the complete and utter disappointment in myself for having allowed this to happen once again.

I was in disbelief that after all the precautions and adjustments in protocol, I was now dealing with the same feelings I'd experienced when both Roxy and Katiti had gone wild. On top of this, I had the added guilt of being confident that Honey Bun was pregnant and now alone in the wild. Horrible scenarios of being cold and hungry—or someone finding, selling, or even killing her—would reduce me to tears whenever I had a private moment. I tried to put on a brave face for staff and friends, but I cried myself to sleep many nights when no one was around.

Occasionally, we would see pangolin tracks near the house, but I finally stopped leaving the house door open at night and hoped she was safe. Another BBC crew came and went, with Amos playing the leading role, and soon word got around that Honey Bun had gone wild. I had no problem that she was on her own because we were preparing her for just that, but I was crushed we had no way to monitor her safety and welfare.

Six long weeks later, my wishes came true, and she returned. A new staff member named Luca, who had been hired only after Honey Bun had escaped, was sitting in his house with the door open after dark, and in walked a pangolin. He immediately radioed me, and every staff member could hear and held their breath as I asked if the pangolin had two holes in her back scale where a tracker had been. I think the local town must have felt the vibrations as whoops of joy resounded from everyone when he confirmed she did.

I left my house at a run, and we met five minutes later in the middle of the bush late at night. The births of my two children were the best days of my life, but holding Honey Bun in my arms again came close. I took her home while whispering over and over how much I loved her. She crawled into bed and promptly fell sound asleep.

Her general veterinary check the next day showed she was healthy and had gained weight. She and Luca quickly bonded, and she started foraging daily with him and returning at night as if she had never been gone.

Only one major change occurred in her evening behavior. Before leaving, she and Amos had slept together. Now she refused to sleep anywhere but with me. She no longer wanted to climb and would wait at the edge of my bed every night to be lifted. Her routine began by sleeping at my feet, and around four am she appeared to get warm and would move near my arm and receive a mini rub while I was still half asleep. From there she would move to just under the pillow next to mine and continue her nap for the day.

I have received some criticism for having Honey Bun sleep in my bed when she chose to. Since I designed and built my home, I incorporated a beautiful pangolin den area near my bedroom, which both Honey Bun and Amos loved, and both have always had the option to visit my sleeping area if they wished. This is not something I offer to other species long-term because, in my opinion, none of the other species I have worked with have needed it. It is not an option for the wild releasable pangolins that come into our center. I argue adamantly that those who have been most critical of this behavior know nothing about raising pangolins from a young age. I believe it is like elephant and rhino surrogate caregivers, who move into the stables with their orphans. The only difference is that pangolins are smaller, so it was much easier to have them move into my specially designed sleeping area. Humans cannot function without sleep, so this practice of allowing Honey Bun and Amos to join me, only if they chose to, was more about proper care than a need to fulfill some personal desire, and this should be clearly understood.

When I felt confident of Honey Bun's pregnancy, I contacted my old friends at BBC and let them know there was a chance she was pregnant. If she was going to give birth, it was an amazing opportunity to share this special event with the world and continue to raise pangolin profiles with some good news, rather than the never-ending news detailing seizures of thousands of tons of dead ones. I had spent almost a year off and on with BBC for the previous film, and I knew I could trust them to be sensitive, committed, and qualified. As expected, they were excited but needed confirmation and a possible due date.

At the time, we were busy building a small clinic and establishing a partnership with our long-term vet to have her on site at least one week a month. Dr. Lyndsay Scott is amazing and one of the kindest, most sensitive, and hardest-working vets I have ever worked with. She arrived with her equipment, Honey Bun willingly allowed the sonar to be moved over her stomach area (just like with humans), and then chaos erupted over the footage as no one was really sure what we were seeing. At first, everyone rejoiced with the news that it looked like a fetus. Then discussion followed that maybe they were mistaken and what was showing was the bladder. Then back to fetus, but not sure. All this confusion was not because the vets were in any way incompetent, and one, in fact, is undoubtedly one of the most experienced with pangolins in southern Africa. It was simply that no one was sure what a pregnant mama's early sonar would look like as no one had ever confirmed one before.

Finally, after another month and a larger suspected fetus, it seemed official, and we believed she was pregnant. Now we just wondered if she was the first ground pangolin in recorded history to get pregnant in captivity, or was it possible that Amos had not mated successfully and she had found a wild male and mated during her six-week escape. We could only answer this question once the baby was born and genetic testing was done, but my gut told me Amos was going to be a papa.

Soon after, a video started going viral on social media. I recognized that my old friend Roxy Dankwerts's organization had filmed the entire birth of a ground pangolin pup. It was so beautiful, and I picked up the phone the second it ended and called the woman I still had never met. Sadly, she told me the mother's milk had never come in, and the baby had not survived. I could hear the desolation in her voice and knew so well the feelings of helplessness and failure she was experiencing. She also noted, as I had with Roxy pangolin, that they had no indication of impending birth until it was taking place.

Each pangolin rescuer I have spent any time with tends to blame him or herself when something goes wrong. We know in our heads that we are pioneers, and the act of discovery can lead to misfortune and mistakes, but our hearts always review what we could have done differently. The death of this pup for no explainable reason made me even more worried about Honey Bun's future. If she was not already the Queen Bee of my household, she soon became one.

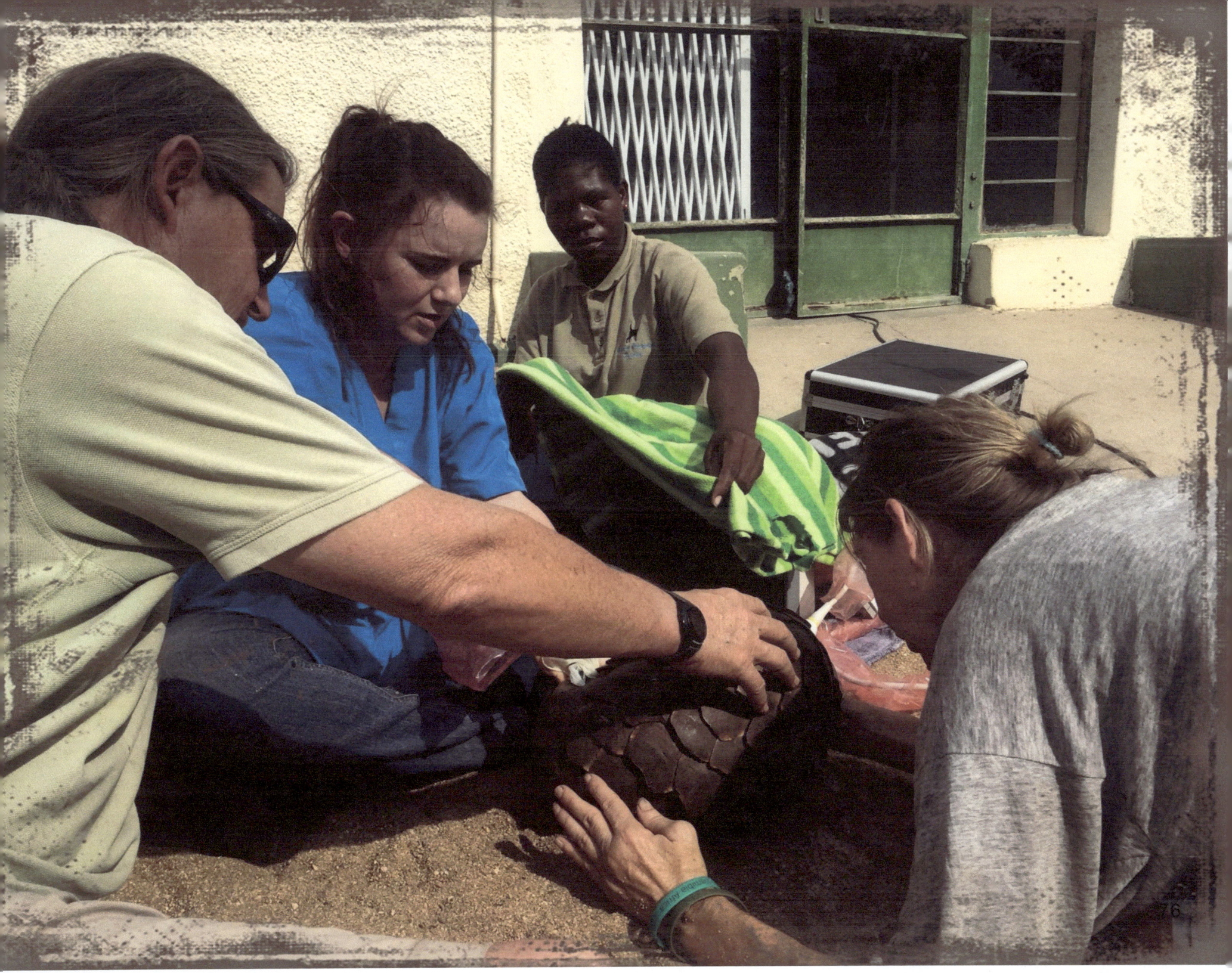

"

Are pangolins smart?

Pangolins are highly intelligent, which is unexpected as commonly a mammal with a small brain in relation to body size indicates less intelligence.

My experience is that pangolins are determined and will try over and over to solve a problem. Once they find the solution, they no longer search for alternatives but repeat it when faced with the same problem. I have watched Katiti, determined to crawl into my bed (before I willingly allowed it), standing before an antique bedside table with thin drawers from top to bottom. He learned he could pull the handle of the fourth drawer (always the same one), open it, climb up on the now opened drawer, and reach for the next one. By repeating the opening of higher drawers, he would reach my bed and promptly fall asleep. Many watched Honey Bun as she opened the refrigerator in the BBC film. This was not something we taught but that she figured out herself. Honey Bun loved a certain canned vet food that most pangolins refuse to eat, and she could obviously smell the can through the fridge. That motivation was enough to teach her a behavior she never forgot, and I had to add a bolt to the refrigerator to keep her out. Similarly, I watched Honey Bun figured out how to open almost any door she could access by reaching for the handle and pushing it down.

Observations as I know them

• Pangolins react to noise or vibrations and if afraid can instantly stand motionless or flatten their bodies to the ground and leopard-crawl to a crevasse or deep bush.

• Pangolins respond to voices they know and trust and will visibly calm when hearing them.

• They can walk up to ten kms a day to find suitable territory. This makes releases difficult because if the new area already has an existing adult, the new pangolin will be chased away. When this consistently happens, the new animal can die of exhaustion and starvation before finding an open territory.

• They will not eat in an area that has recently been visited by another ant-eating species, such as aardvark or aardwolf, and I believe this can cause weight loss and eventual death in drought conditions.

• Pangolins love to roll in mud and water, but only if they feel completely secure. The duration ranges between three to fifteen minutes. This behavior could be ascribed to cooling off, preventing parasites, or masking scent for defence. I believe all three play a roll, but I also believe they enjoy themselves. Every pangolin I observed had renewed vigor and an increased appetite once they came out of the water.

- Pangolins will also roll in other animal urine or feces if fresh, and I believe this is more an effort to mask their scent from predators and maybe a parasite control mechanism.

- Pangolins enjoy playing. Katiti often played with my shoes or other animal species in rehabilitation that he had bonded with.

- Pangolins are very clean animals and will often use their long tongue to lick between their scales.

"

Can pangolins be kept in captivity?

This is an incredibly controversial topic because as pangolins become better known, there is a new trend to find ways to use them for tourism. When done ethically and with the interest of the animal as a core principle, I have no problem with the concept, but the reality creates problems.

REST ran a tourism operation for years without a pangolin in sight. However, since we have become recognized as a center focusing on their care, many visitors come hoping to see a live one. Our operating principle remains that no pangolin will ever be kept solely for the purpose of tourism, and their health and welfare will never be intentionally compromised for anything.

There is no doubt that both Katiti and Honey Bun were able to calm wild pangolins that came in for rehabilitation, when it was suitable for them to meet. I believe they communicated to the frightened animals that they were safe, and their pheromones would have emphasized they felt safe and secure, which could only have relaxed the new pangolins. But neither were ever kept solely for that purpose.

There was also an unexpected result of raising pangolin pups. Due to the fact that REST also raised other orphaned species, it was not unusual for the others to follow along on our daily pangolin walks. This gives babies of any species the knowledge and courage to survive in the bush and was vital to REST's principles of captivity in preparation for wild life. Katiti grew fond of one particular warthog, and Honey Bun was often joined by a sweet meerkat.

Difficulties arise when tourism operators (even very good ones) don't understand a pangolin is very different from other species. Even if in the wild with a tracker, the continuous and persistent following of the individual can cause unseen harm and often eventual death. We still cannot explain this phenomenon, but both researchers and bush guides have recorded instances in which what appeared to be a healthy individual, seemingly accustomed to human contact, suddenly died for no explainable reason. Therefore, we recently decided that daily visitors will not be allowed close viewing of any wild pangolin being monitored by us.

Most of my conservation colleagues also allow no or limited public access to their pangolins. However, I firmly believe that a few circumstances do justify human visitors having restricted access to see a live pangolin. Education is vital to long-term conservation as it creates interest, awareness, and critical funding, but it is all about balance and welfare of the animal. Our current protocols are very strict.

85

If we have a non-releasable or long-term care pangolin that is not stressed with limited public contact, then the following rules apply:

Physical contact is not allowed, visitors and guides must remain absolutely quiet, no camera flashes are allowed, the pangolin remains with the handler or on the ground, and no one may stand or move in front of a pangolin as this disturbs their food source and makes feeding impossible. Pictures become less important than the experience, and taxidermied pangolins on display play a vital role so that discussions and physical interaction can take place away from the live animal.

Visitors still leave caring, with more knowledge, and with a renewed hope that we can prevent the extinction of pangolins. Amos was a perfect example of an animal that could allow visitors to fall in love with the species while causing no mental or physical harm to him. He was a non-releasable animal, comfortable around humans, and behaved like a wild pangolin when in the bush.

Researchers are no exception to potentially harming the species they care so much about. Sometimes it occurs out of neglect, but often with pangolins it is accidentally done simply out of a lack of knowledge, making information dissemination critical. One researcher shared a story with me from when she released a strong, healthy male in a territory she believed was loosely held by another adult male, thinking the space was big enough to accommodate them both. She watched as a fight ensued and immediately checked the new male but found no obvious injuries. However, soon after she found him dead, and the postmortem showed extensive internal damage. This was a tragic event, but in my opinion, it would be even more tragic if no lesson was learned from it. Too often these cases are not shared for fear of blame.

Researchers can also fall into the trap of putting unsuitable trackers on animals in order to research them. Some mean well, others just want the prestigious data, but I would rather have no data than compromise the health or welfare of an animal. This is one of the major reasons why Honey Bun had not yet been officially released in the wild. We were waiting until a suitable tracker was designed that would ensure her safety without compromising foraging, mating, and motherhood.

A few years ago, a well-known film crew choose not to film with colleagues in South Africa because their visitation policies were too strict. They instead filmed with a new and inexperienced pangolin researcher, and it was unsuccessful for a variety of reasons—and I suspect caused major stress to the wild pangolin mother and her pup. While research, filming, and education are vital, pangolins need to be handled much more sensitively than any other species I have worked with.

As an alternative to live viewing, REST is finalizing a 360 film experience that will allow visitors to take a virtual walk with a pangolin. Special 360 cameras were used to film the daily activities of our pangolins in the bush, and it is an amazing experience, even for someone like me who has had countless opportunities to follow pangolins. The visitor wears goggles, and the world becomes a 360 reality. If you physically move your head to the left, you can see Honey Bun walking toward you, and as she passes, if you look to the right, you will see her moving away. Look up and any birds flying over have been caught on film, and the trees can be seen blowing in the wind. It is an achievable concept, and one I have asked numerous zoos to sponsor.

To date no one has agreed that their visitors would be interested in such an experience, but maybe the changes that COVID-19 has brought to the world will finally initiate this program. It's a waiting game, and one in which REST is a professional. For years no large film production company was interested in filming pangolins, even when I offered the opportunity after Katiti was born. However, once BBC had successfully led the effort, others became interested, so I am hopeful for the future of our 360 film experience plan. Historically, the zoo community has led some of the greatest success stories on endangered species by developing veterinary and welfare treatment for young, sick, or injured animals.

Life in captivity has proven difficult for the tree pangolin species and impossible for both the giant and ground pangolins. REST is not perfect, has made mistakes in the past, and I have no doubt will make more in the future, but the hardest inconsistency is that we are not able to determine why some efforts succeed with one pangolin but fail on others. It sometimes feels like a game of luck, and the scientist in me is frustrated while my conservation side becomes heartbroken.

One of the greatest problems facing all pangolin species is that, unlike most of their endangered counterparts, very few of the species have ever been successfully held or bred in captivity. Rhino, elephant, and tiger have had holding and breeding successes on private reserves and national parks, but pangolins have had no such luck. If they do go extinct in the wild, it will be final! Extinction is a very big word and one we need to realize has immense ramifications.

I cannot say what the ideal scenario is, but I do believe we must take great care and ask difficult questions with no easy answers. Part of my objective in writing this book is to begin an open discussion and determine best methods that allow pangolins to be pangolins while educating the world about their uniqueness. I believe that if you can completely commit mentally, physically, and financially to saving pangolins, and you study and put into operation the latest, most ethical protocols without thought to financial gain, then you should be given a chance. If just one of those elements is missing, then please do not even touch a pangolin as too many are going to suffer at your hands. Armchair conservationists should stay seated and quiet as they seldom know as much as they think they do and often cause more harm than good.

It is hard to explain the raising and rehabilitation process of a pangolin to someone who has not attempted it. The dedication and sacrifice long-term are like no other animal I can imagine. Their sensitivity to everything, lack of proven veterinary and rehabilitation protocols, and ability to curl up in a ball so tight that forced feeding without sedatives is impossible makes care extremely difficult. They need constant attention and long-term bonding, which makes loving them physically and emotionally draining—and losing them absolutely devastating. One wakes every day wondering if today is the day you will make a mistake that will cost them their life. They seem fine one day and the next are at death's door, fighting for their life with little prior warning.

I have heard this story time and time again from everyone who has attempted to raise a young one. I have yet to discover why so many young pangolins die suddenly. When that breakthrough is understood, it will be a major achievement, and I will be insanely grateful for the discoverer's contribution.

If you are fortunate enough to encounter a pangolin in the wild, my strict advice is: Do not pick it up, move it to another location, kneel next to it, or take pictures of it in your arms unless absolutely vital for the interests of the animal's safety.

Take a picture as it walks by and hold in your memory that you were fortunate enough to see one of the coolest animals alive in the wild. If a tourism company is offering pangolin sightings, research them carefully. If the animal has a tracking device on it, there is a good chance this poor animal is being visited every day. For such shy creatures, that is life-threatening, and the animal is being used only for financial gain.

If you find an injured pangolin or someone is offering to sell you one, call the police, nature conservation authorities, or a well-respected pangolin organization. I have negotiated with many poachers and received calls from all over Africa, which I have been able to advise on or direct to colleagues in other countries. Keeping a wild pangolin in your home overnight is dangerous as any chemicals, floor cleaners, or pesticides (including mosquito repellent residues) can be absorbed through its feet and possibly cause harm, not to mention the pangolin can climb and destroy just about anything and they are especially susceptible to the cold.

If captive breeding is ever successful, it will be so unique as to be practically, economically, and scientifically impossible on even a small scale. Each pangolin requires extreme dedication, perseverance, and funding, and even organizations completely dedicated will sometimes, if not often, experience failures. Simply put, holding pangolins will never make a person wealthy. The investment and percentage of failure far exceeds the financial benefits for captive breeding, tourism, or personal interest.

"

Pangolin evolution

Pangolins are one of the oldest living creatures, and their existence goes back 80 million years, while early humans are only 7 million years old. Some date them back to the dinosaurs (they certainly walk like a mini T. rex), and recent genetic research argues they are most closely related to the large cats of Africa. Their name derives from the Malay word "pengguling," which loosely translates to "something that rolls up." I find it horrific an animal that does absolutely no harm to people and has existed for millennia is under dire threat. Many predict pangolins could be extinct within a decade or less.

- The ground pangolin and giant pangolin are the only species that are bipedal, walking predominantly on their hind feet. Most of the time their front legs are slightly crossed and held just below their chin. They will sometimes place their front feet on the ground, and this usually happens when they wake, are tired, or are going up or downhill. It makes sense they would not want to wear down their sharp front claws as these are essential for digging. When walking, they hold their tail up about four cm off the ground. For years I shared public information that the best way to track a pangolin was to find the spoor of all four feet and marks from the dragging tail because that is what the books said. I now know that if they are dragging their tail, it is a sure sign of severe weakness and usually means they have less than 24 hours to live.

- Their feet are very similar to elephants and tortoises, and while soft as a pup, they become callused over time and can walk in almost any environment.

- None of my observations have led me to conclude they have a right or left hand preference when either walking or digging.

- Pangolins roll in a ball when threatened, with their tail overlapping their body for protection.

93

• The tail has an unknown number of muscles in it, but when curled in a defensive ball by a healthy adult pangolin has so far proven to be impossible to open by humans and most predators (or remove from my leg).

• They have a very soft-skinned stomach area with no proper hair anywhere on the body, except for short, dense hair over parts of their face.

• They can see but probably use their developed sense of smell for most activity.

• A healthy pangolin has clear, dark eyes and a moist nose.

• They have a sticky mucus on their tongue, which probably protects the tongue and aids in capturing ants and termites before swallowing. Usually it extends straight, but very seldom it seems to get curled up and twisted during extending.

• A pangolin laps up water with its tongue, extending and contracting the tongue with each lap.

94

• Their tongue is not only used for eating and drinking, but is also extended when needing to smell (such as being introduced to a new person or situation).

• Often in death a pangolin's tongue will extend out of its mouth. It is not known exactly why, but the sure sign of a very sick pangolin is if any tongue is exposed and not retracted.

• To defecate/urinate, pangolins dig a hole with their front feet, pushing the dirt through their back legs into a small mound. They then crouch over the hole and when finished drag their tail over the pile of dirt behind their feet as they walk away. This covers the hole, and they usually remain clean. The female arches her back during the process, and the male tends to do more of a squat. I believe this is done to cover their scent and have never seen any other variation but have heard reliable reports of pangolins defecating in their burrows, peeing occasionally as a possible scent mark, and even reports of males occasionally lifting their legs. If that does in fact happen, I have never witnessed it.

• Their scales are not bulletproof, as sometimes reported, and I can confirm this firsthand having cared for a pangolin shot with a bullet we could not remove as it was lodged in the spine.

• They are very susceptible to cold as their scales do not insolate them as well as hair or fur.

• Pangolins usually use dens already made by warthog and aardvark. When entering the existing den, they will almost always dig a little deeper at the back before falling asleep. These dens tend to be warmer and more humid than the outside conditions. They like unused dens, which means they often emerge full of spiderwebs.

• Most ground pangolins do not climb trees, but I have witnessed fewer than ten events over the years. Their climbing method is to put both front arms around the tree, push up with their back legs, and grip higher with their front legs again—like a palm tree climber. Compared to tree pangolins, however, they are clumsy and uncoordinated when climbing.

• Namibian pangolins are not solely nocturnal, especially in winter. We experience our main summer rainfalls as early as October, usually ending by March. During the winter months of June-August, the ground is hard, and the nights can be cold. Ants stay deeper underground and only rise to the surface during the warmer daylight hours. As a result of the rock-hard winter soil, pangolins forage during the day as they would expend too much energy if they had to dig deep in the cold night. As a result, most pangolin sightings occur during the winter season when the pangolins wake around noon and the seasonal grasses are not as high.

• There have been reports of pangolins swimming, but I believe this is very uncommon in Namibia. The behavior may only occur in certain individuals that have learned to cross rivers or dams to access other food sources. Physically, they are not designed to be good swimmers, and in fact I do know of one video taken in my presence where the pangolin appeared to be swimming, but the pool was very shallow. The pangolin was gliding over the ground rather than swimming.

• They love mud, which may be good for cooling themselves and protecting their scales or scent.

"

Research

Historically, very few people or organizations have managed to document reliable observations about pangolins—most arguably because pangolins are very shy and seldom exhibit normal behavior when followed by a human. I have pleaded with manufacturers for years to develop a small, sturdy, reliable, and long-lasting satellite unit. Designing for pangolins is apparently very difficult, so I continue to use only small VHF units.

In my opinion, all the current cell or satellite trackers are too large and heavy for Namibia's smaller pangolins. I learned early in my success of fitting satellite trackers to vultures how much more is learned with advanced technology, but the equipment itself should not risk an animal's health and welfare.

The African Pangolin Working Group (APWG) based in South Africa has been a research and anti-poaching leader in our region and works alongside the Johannesburg Wildlife Veterinary Hospital, which I believe is the best in Africa on handling severe cases. Dr. Karin Lourens and rehabilitation specialist Nicci Wright have led the development of clinical protocols for analyzing blood, tube feeding, and medications best suited for pangolins. I will always be grateful for their support in some of our most critical cases. It is now considered ill-informed and unethical to release any pangolin without blood analysis and proper treatment for stress, parasites, and dehydration.

Blood analysis is a huge breakthrough in pangolin care, and while time and experience may change some of the techniques and baseline data, treatment is becoming more scientific and thus easier to repeat and quantify. One of the most satisfying days of my life was when well-known rhino specialists Grant and his brother Dr. William Foulds received permission from one of their sponsors, Abaxis, to loan us an incredibly expensive and essential blood-testing machine.

Usually, the research community argues that a proven science should be based on a reliable and repeatable sample size of at least twenty. We are far from establishing many scientific facts with pangolins as most of the examples I have referred to are a sample size of between one and ten.

This forces conservationists and researchers to work within these "non-scientific" parameters out of necessity, and many books rely on unpublished data and field observations. While the REST team has worked diligently to find answers for care, nursing, and veterinary procedures of ground pangolins, we still have more questions than answers. Even with these new protocols, it will never be easy.

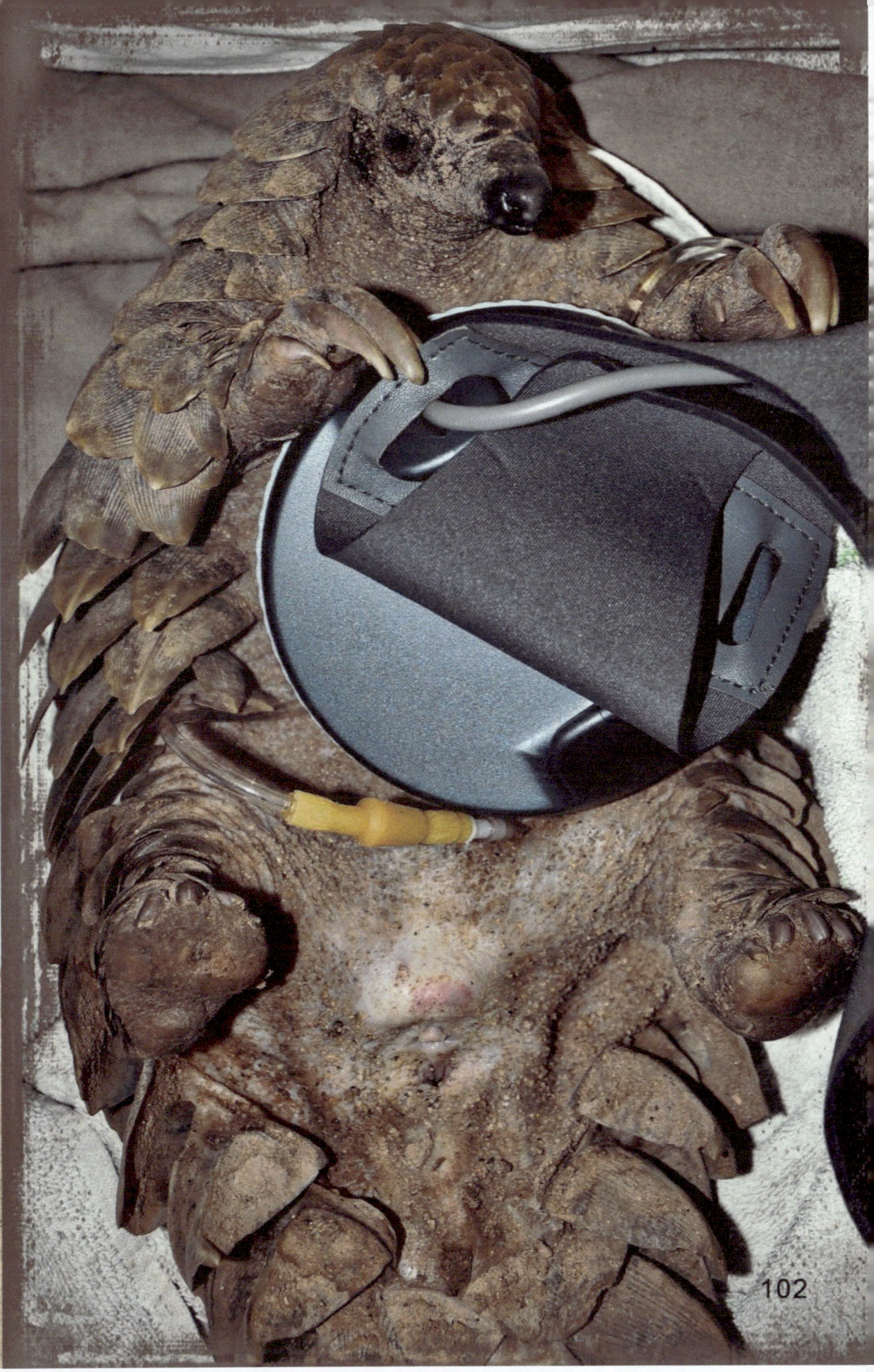

"

2020 – The worst year of my life

As the new 2020 year began, REST was doing great. Our UK team was developing FoREST as a donation path through REST's Max's Rescue Ranger Project, we had several excellent employees, our center was developing, we expected a baby from Honey Bun, and we were close to opening our new camping site to become less dependent on donations. In March, as the world began to understand the ramifications of COVID-19, REST closed its gates to protect our pangolins and staff.

We took no visitors, my staff went into self-imposed lockdown, we stocked up on animal and human food, planted a huge garden, and dedicated ourselves to the animals. Our overseas staff left on the last flights out, and we prayed for the best but prepared for the worst.

We realized the drought was negatively affecting our pangolins, and reports were all over the media of wild ones in human areas searching desperately for food. Honey Bun and Amos started losing weight, and I believe this is when Honey Bun aborted her baby without her walker even realizing.

Pangolins usually defecate and urinate at the same time within about fifteen minutes of waking. Our walkers have been trained to collect feces samples when possible, but sometimes the pangolin is moving too quickly or for some other reason they don't find time to stop and collect.

Since we could never confirm 100% that Honey Bun was pregnant, we will never know for sure. But once she had died, her postmortem ovaries did show she could have been pregnant, and drought and effects of her illness could have caused a natural abortion.

Which brings me to some of the hardest moments in my life.

On June 3, 2020, we rushed Amos to a nearby vet when his glucose levels dropped. It was a bit chaotic, with an expert pangolin vet from another country on the phone advising several wonderful vets without much pangolin experience as they desperately tried to raise his blood sugar levels and stabilize his breathing.

When finished, I wrapped him in a blanket, thanking God and the vets for a job well done. As I looked again, I realized he had just left this world. I searched for answers and blamed myself for not knowing what had gone wrong.

Unfortunately, a postmortem done by the vet showed no conclusive cause of death, which made losing him even worse, but the stress at the clinic probably added to his death. I spoke with many for theories—and some agree and others not—but my instinct tells me the overall cause had something to do with the drought. I still suspect, but have not proven, that the ants affected by drought were producing formic acid quicker and in larger doses to protect their dwindling colonies. Our pangolins, like their wild counterparts, were just not getting enough of a wild diet and/or were ingesting some natural toxins, leading to organ complications and environmental stress.

Almost a year earlier, the first recorded black-bellied pangolin to be raised, released, and monitored by the Sangha Pangolin Project also died, and they grieved the sudden loss of their beloved "Pangy." A new parasite was later discovered, which they believe caused her death. This type of research can take months and sometimes years but slowly builds a picture that answers questions.

Within a month of losing Amos, Honey Bun began showing similar signs of distress. This time we caught the subtle symptoms very early and started treating her immediately. The additional stress associated with Amos's vet visit lingered in our minds, so we began intensive consultations with Dr. Karin Lourens and used her protocols to test blood, tube feed, and alleviate as much stress as possible. Honey Bun would respond positively to the treatment, and then her glucose levels would crash again, forcing us to perform emergency procedures and bring her back from the brink of death.

Dr. Lourens suspected an ulcer, which we began to treat, but we could not find anyone in Namibia with a small enough endoscope (tiny camera that is put down the throat to investigate the stomach) to confirm the ulcer. My staff mastered her care with the least possible stress, but after another glucose drop, we decided Honey Bun could receive better care in South Africa, as they had more expertise and better equipment than anyone in Namibia.

At this point, COVID-19 prevented any normal cross-border travel, but we began applying for the export and import permits as I searched for a travel solution. Our social media appeals attracted a local airfreight company called Bay Air, and they offered, free of charge, a dedicated flight as soon as we received the permits. Honey Bun would be fetched with a local plane, taken to the transport plane, and within hours would be in the vet's care. I could not travel with her due to COVID-19 bans on any travel, and that broke my heart, but I knew it was the best option available.

Unfortunately, this process became long and political, and the Namibian government required me to bring her to a Windhoek vet, who would determine the necessity of leaving for South Africa. They made it clear she would now be the responsibility of others, and I no longer had any say over her care.

When a government official informed me that I must hand Honey Bun over, it was late evening so I had one last night with her before the long trip to Windhoek. I lay with Honey Bun and told her I would understand if she chose to join Amos. I knew I had failed her, and that guilt, whether real or imagined, took me to a breaking point. Fortunately, my daughter had rushed to my side and became my lifeline. Until my dying day, I will always be grateful to the Windhoek vet for not only making huge personal sacrifices to care for Honey Bun, but for allowing me to stay with her as she acknowledged our bond, my commitment, and my expertise. My daughter and I moved into a little guesthouse, and Honey Bun was allowed to return home with us between the vet visits three times a day.

Everyone involved felt that if we could get a pangolin blood transfusion, Honey Bun could hold out a bit longer for the permits and flight. Dr. Lourens in South Africa had the blood but no permit to get it couriered to us, and we had the pangolin but no permit to send her to South Africa. Frustration cannot explain how distraught I was. We began searching Namibia for any nearby pangolin with a tracker as a once-off blood donor, but only one could be found so quickly and the researcher chose not to allow the field operation. As with any procedure, there were risks involved. Even though we had assurances from three vets that it would not harm the wild pangolin, I respected the decision, even though I did not agree with it.

105

After an excruciating time delay, it was finally decided Honey Bun would be allowed to travel to South Africa, but unfortunately the weekend was approaching and the governments on both sides shut down. The Namibians managed to rush through an export permit late Friday evening, but the South African government could only convene the following Monday, which meant the earliest we could fly would be Tuesday.

On Monday, July 6, the vet messaged me to see if Honey Bun was still alive for our six am round of injections. The night before, in desperation, she had received a dog blood transfusion and had been expected to reject the blood immediately but had survived.

As I lay looking at my suffering girl, I once again told her it was okay if she left, but that I prayed she would hold on for the flight. Moments later, she took her last breath, and my world collapsed. Before I could even morn for her, news of her death was shared by others, so I managed a heartfelt RIP on social media, took her body to the vet for a postmortem, and then handed her remains to government officials, as required by law.

News of her death travelled the world, and while I never responded to all the memorable, sincere, and kind messages that came in, they meant so much to me. I have read them many times. I did respond to two messages of criticism that she had been made a pet as this was not the case and needed a clear response.

The concept of a wildlife blood bank to honor Honey Bun came to me within hours. I am sure it was my mind and soul's way of handling the devastation of her loss. It focused me and culminated in an amazing art fundraiser. Unfortunately, there were a few people who found any fault they could with the concept and began to attack REST. Why, I still do not know as my policy has always been live and let live. I have always welcomed the idea of other pangolin facilities working "in conjunction" and not "in competition" with REST.

The coordinated attacks brought me into a very low personal space, so I temporarily left the farm in good hands and visited the sea because, for the first time in almost a decade, I didn't have a pangolin to care for.

It was there-after weeks of eating, sleeping, and healing-that I could finally finish this book and in the process realize that because I know my actions for pangolins have always been honest, selfless, and sincere, I am happy with myself. I finally realized that discovery can result in failures, but that any feeling of failure as a person could only happen if I allowed it. I decided I would not.

Upon reflection, I think Honey Bun chose to stay alive during our time in Windhoek to protect me and REST's reputation. She was under certified vet care, and a proper postmortem was immediately conducted. The results took months due to COVID-19 limitations, but we recently received the results noting that Honey Bun had two major underlying problems. The first was a severe ulcer that had not yet ruptured but was life-threatening. We may never be able to prove the original cause, but I am sure it had to do with the drought and possibly ant formic acid.

Information received from another organization in Namibia studying pangolins that year confirms they also witnessed many pangolin deaths and felt the drought was the major or at least a large contributing factor. At least one vet I highly respect disagrees, and she may be right, but her theory that Honey Bun was under stress due to her captivity does not makes sense for several reasons:

• Other vets have commented that an ulcer should typically take months to develop. If her stress was due to captivity, why only manifest itself after four years in my care?

• If for some reason the ulcer had been a long-standing condition, why had she only lost weight once the drought had started? Perhaps the ulcer was triggered by the drought.

• Additionally, the fact that two of our long-term care pangolins died with in a month of each other seemed more than coincidence, and the postmortem tests did not show any artificial poisons or typical pangolin stress signs, such as major lung damage, on either of them.

All the vets I have conferred with agree that Honey Bun's immediate cause of death was the ulcer. She could have possibly been saved with intensive treatment, but that was not her only health issue.

The second was a very rare form of cancer. It is called hemangiosarcoma and can be found as an internal or external form. I was originally advised that hers had spread internally, but further investigation showed she had two lesions on her skin, which are removable for prolonged life but usually still fatal.

Quite honestly, she is gone, but I will spend the rest of my life searching for answers to prevent further pangolin deaths. If mistakes are ever proven, I will take full responsibility. Hopefully, proof of some kind will be discovered that furthers our knowledge, but for now I am taking time to morn, reflect, and write.

Grieving made me take a good look at my life. I realized it was completely out of balance, caring for Honey Bun and Amos.

There was even a young woman in 2019 doing research on the pressures that pangolin people experience and how this affects their psychological, physical, and social well-being. I have spoken with many pangolin frontline experts in Africa, and all agree that in many ways our lives are not balanced. Even though everyone is intelligent, dedicated, happy, and mentally stable, I do not know one pangolin caregiver who does not recognize the problems.

Personally, I had almost no social life, rarely ate good meals at night, slept odd hours, and was constantly searching for extra funds needed to support our work. In addition, I neglected building and strengthening relationships with government officials, which allowed others to spread false information without me countering it or even knowing it was happening. I cared too much about what others thought of my work. Unfounded criticism would cut me to the core and could often make me physically ill. I simply wanted to be left in peace to work with the animals and not bother nor be bothered with others. That all said, I honestly could tell anyone that up until 2020 I was the happiest woman alive. It is now up to me to rebuild my spirit, and this book is one avenue toward achieving that goal.

Two years AD Honey Bun, and my book is finally finished. REST managed to adapt to COVID-19 conditions, and visitors, volunteers, and students began contacting us again. But sadly, REST's existence became political. We were raided by the government, and twenty years of research samples were taken, including over a million Namibian dollars' worth of pangolin scales held for research purposes and reported yearly to the government. The government never gave REST a proper inventory list of all that was taken, and many believe corruption was involved. After a year of trying to "work through the system" with no income or official government response to our future, I finally went public with the situation. After another half a year of complete stonewalling, I decided to move REST's base to an international platform, rather than fight my own country for the chance to do their conservation work. We hope to open our gates to visitors once again, but there will be changes. Namibian tourism relied too heavily on overseas visitors, so REST is thinking out of the box about what and how we can keep caring for animals.

I can only be sure of one thing. The principles REST was founded on will never change because they are honest and true. How the REST team will make our way forward is still developing, but our core values of helping animals in need and releasing them in the wild when possible will never change. Especially not because others are jealous, unethical, or complacent.

I hope that while reading this adventure we have shared smiles and tears. It is my story of pangolins in my life, and while moments have been heartbreaking, most of it was one of adventure, hope, gratitude—and especially love. I hope to see the day when "observations" will be facts. Whether I have been correct or incorrect in my theories, I will rejoice in the new knowledge because while this is my story, its purpose is to save pangolins.

When a pangolin cries...

"Once upon a time,
The pangolin roamed the earth,
But sadly they will be no more,
There's none left to give birth."
This might be what you'll tell your kids,
As they might never see.
We vanished due to sick beliefs.
One wouldn't let us be.

We now lead the endangered list,
As most hunted of all.
We do no harm, we just do good.
Why do we have to fall?
Being part of nature's cycle,
With a vital role to play,
Why don't you humans help us?
We have no voice to say.

Our scales, of use to only us,
All other beliefs are wrong.
Till when will we get killed for them?
Been going on too long.
The scales meant for protection,
Our downfall they became.
The most trafficked on the planet
Now our claim to fame.

All forces of nature and all other beasts,
For those we have no fears,
But humans, you we cannot fight.
Do you not see our tears?
Oh, it was you who put us
Right where we are here today.
That you now hear and save us,
We beg you and we pray.

We don't deserve what we've been dealt,
The cruelty we have to face.
And all this has been caused by greed.
Yes, by the "human" race.
Many good hearts out there
Do bleed for us and are so very sore,
But only actions will bring change,
Or soon we'll be no more.

We want to live. We want to breathe.
We just want to be free.
The plea is that you help us.
That's where our spirit yearns to be.

—Harald Bartsch

The end

Photo credits

Cover - Scott & Judy Hurd Photography
Pg 2 - Scott & Judy Hurd Photography
Pg 3 - Scott & Judy Hurd Photography
Pg 4 - Scott & Judy Hurd Photography
Pg 6 - Scott & Judy Hurd Photography
Pg 7 - 1 Algemeine Zeitung Namibia
Pg 7 - 3 Indie Hookins 9 years old – Paulette Hookins
Pg 8 - 1 Zane Ackermann 4 ½ years old – Rebecca Ackermann
Pg 8 - 2 Jeffrey Ginsberg
Pg 8 - 3,4 Varta Batteries
Pg 8 - 5 Issak age 9
Pg 8 - 6 Artist Kisieia Garcia, "Honour her presence"
Pg 8 - 7 FoREST & Max's Rescue Rangers fundraiser
Pg 10 - 1 Pham Van Thong, Save Vietnam's Wildlife
Pg 10 - 2 Yohindrau Balakrishnaa
Pg 10 - 3 Rajesh, Nandankanan Zoo, India
Pg 10 - 4 Madhu Sabbavarapu, Eastern Ghats of South India
Pg 10 - 6 Jacha Potgieter, Sangha Lodge, Central African Republic
Pg 10 - 7 Ruth H Smith, Agence Nationals des Parcs Nationaux Gabon
Pg 11 - 2 unknown
Pg 14 - 4 Stretch Combrink, Living desert snake park
Pg 21 - 2 Okonjima
Pg 22 - Okonjima
Pg 23 - 1 Scott & Judy Hurd Photography
Pg 31 - 1 Scott & Judy Hurd Photography
Pg 39 - Diagramed by Dr. Karin Lourens, Johannesburg Wildlife
      Veterinary Hospital
Pg 40 - 1, 2, 3, Dr. Debbie English, Provet Wildlife Services &
        Animal Hospital – Diagrammed by Dr. Kelsey Skinner
Pg 42 - 2 Scott & Judy Hurd Photography

Pg 44 - 3 Scott & Judy Hurd Photography
Pg 54 - 3 Scott & Judy Hurd Photography
Pg 76 - unknown
Pg 79 - all Scott & Judy Hurd Photography
Pg 86 - unknown
Pg 90 - Christian Boix Photography
Pg 94 - 1 unknown
Pg 97 - 5 Carol Smith
Pg 102 - 1 unknown

*All other photos taken by Maria Diekmann

www.ingramcontent.com/pod-product-compliance
Lightning Source LLC
Chambersburg PA
CBHW040819120626

46551CB00005B/607